THE MIGHTY HEALER

THE MIGHTY HEALER

Thomas Holloway's Victorian Patent Medicine Empire

Verity Holloway

PEN & SWORD HISTORY

First published in Great Britain in 2016 by
Pen & Sword History
an imprint of
Pen & Sword Books Ltd
47 Church Street
Barnsley
South Yorkshire
S70 2AS

ISBN 978 1 4738 5 5670

Typeset in 11.5 pt Ehrhardt MT by
Replika Press Pvt Ltd, India
Printed and bound by CPI UK

Pen & Sword Books Ltd incorporates the imprints of Pen & Sword
Archaeology, Atlas, Aviation, Battleground, Discovery, Family History,
History, Maritime, Military, Naval, Politics, Railways, Select, Transport,
True Crime, Fiction, Frontline Books, Leo Cooper, Praetorian Press,
Seaforth Publishing and Wharncliffe.

For a complete list of Pen & Sword titles please contact
PEN & SWORD BOOKS LIMITED
47 Church Street, Barnsley, South Yorkshire S70 2AS, England
E-mail: enquiries@pen-and-sword.co.uk
Website: www.pen-and-sword.co.uk

For my dad, Peter Holloway
Nil desperandum

Contents

Introduction

If you took a stroll to Professor Holloway's pill and ointment shop at the far end of London's Strand during the 1860s, you might have witnessed a miracle.

Stepping into the shop, you take your place alongside fretting mothers with colicky babies, old men with old wounds playing up in the damp, and pimply young things hoping for cleaner blood and a stronger constitution. It's a long shop, with a narrow counter running the length of it, at which sit a number of men in aprons occupied in the rolling of pills and the spreading of ointment. The air is oily and spicy, like the apothecaries of old, putting you in mind of miracle-working medicinal plants from exotic climes. Holloway is a learned man, a professor, they say. A professor of what, though, you aren't sure. The advertisements in the daily papers – and there are plenty, so many that Charles Dickens himself has joked about Holloway's ubiquity – depict the shuffling sick appealing to a bearded physician in a toga. Is he Hippocrates or Holloway? What does it matter? *'Every good nurse recommends Holloway's pills!'* But you see no nurses in the shop, only the smartly turned out young men taking the money and doling out the wares. Your ailment itself is of little concern; the cure is always the same. Choose a ceramic pot, large or small, beautifully adorned with the Greek goddess Hygeia, who looks reassuringly like the mother figure of Britannia.

THE MIGHTY HEALER!! Possessed of this great remedy, every man may be his own Doctor; it may be rubbed into the system so as to reach any internal complaint: it even penetrates thc boues, as salt docs meat: by these means it cures the most hidden wounds, such as sores or ulcers in the throat, stomach, liver, abdomen, spine, or other parts. It is an infallible remedy for bad legs, bad breasts, contracted or stiff joints, gout, rheumatism, and all skin diseases.

You cannot help but feel in safe hands. An assistant fills your chosen pot with herbal-smelling unguent and advises you to apply it wherever and whenever you feel necessary. In dire cases, take up to nine pills a day to cleanse the blood and sharpen the mind. Disregard the medical profession with their exorbitant bills and sneering ways. Thanks to Thomas Holloway, health is within the grasp of the ordinary man, at last.

While you wait, a moustachioed man enters the shop with a sober companion. There is nothing to mark them out among your fellow shoppers until the first man pushes past you into the centre of the shop and spreads his arms as if to give a speech. The room falls into silence. Only then does he spring into the space in front of the counter and proceed to dance around the shop. He laughs wildly and waves his arms, high-kicking to a polka only he can hear. The grasshopper dance forces you and your fellow customers to the corners of the room. His companion looks on, stony-faced.

'You don't know me?' asks the dancing man. 'You don't recognise me?'

A shop assistant ventures out to deal with the lunatic, muttering something about not having had the pleasure.

Pirouetting, the stranger throws an arm to indicate his astonished audience.

Do none of those recognise me? I don't wonder at it! When I was last in this shop, I was carried in on the cabman's back – couldn't walk a step – bad legs of forty years' standing! But now, thanks to your invaluable pills and ointment – look here! And here!

He takes another turn on the dance floor. The tricksters then, in their own words, run for their lives.

It was a prank, of course, and not an uncommon one. The man with the miraculous legs was Edmund Yates, owner and editor of society paper *The World*. Yates, like so many educated Victorians, knew that Professor Holloway's celebrated pills and ointments contained approximately nothing of medicinal value. You might as well have eaten the packaging.

Yet for the working and middle classes of Victorian Britain, my cousin Thomas Holloway's name was as familiar as Boots the Chemists and WH Smith. For sore heads, ulcerated legs, cranky livers, and – let us be delicate – *female troubles*, Holloway's celebrated pills and ointment were a market leviathan. The 'Hollowayian system' of medicine promised to get straight to the source of discomfort and lift the working man back on his feet when no doctor was affordable or trustworthy. Hospitals, after all, were where you went to die. For a shilling, health was to be had by all. Thousands of testimonials couldn't be wrong.

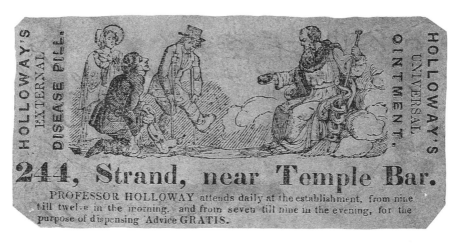

1. A typical Holloway's Pills and Ointment advertisement.
(Wellcome Library, London)

A straightforward rogue, then. Another nineteenth-century charlatan happy to exploit the desperation of the sick. But Thomas Holloway was a man of strange contradictions. He made a vast fortune out of quackery, and he spent it lavishly – not on himself, but on the improvement of the nation. Holloway College for the education of women. Holloway Sanatorium for the humane treatment of the mentally ill. These massive edifices still exist today, along with the staggeringly expensive art collection Thomas purchased for the public to enjoy. There were those who ranked him amongst 'the greatest benefactors of humanity in this or any other age'. Others saw him as an amoral opportunist reaping a tax on gullibility, living in a luxurious Surrey mansion while his customers turned to his products for a cure that didn't exist.

So who was Professor Holloway? How did the son of a humble Cornish publican become one of the wealthiest self-made men in the British Empire? How did his name become known as far away as Egypt as that of a 'healing genius' with medicines 'never known to fail'?

Chapter 1

Spoiling Mother's Coppers

Nowadays, when you walk past The Turk's Head pub in Cornwall's Penzance, you probably won't notice the black plaque marking the childhood home of a 'philanthropist and visionary'.

The pub reputedly dates from the thirteenth century when the Turks sailed over from Jerusalem to invade Penzance. With a smugglers' tunnel in the cellar and at least two priest holes, The Turk's Head is imbued with history and adventure. As a childhood home, it was a place full of ghosts and stories for Thomas and his younger siblings, Mary Jane and Henry. But it was also a place of hard work. For generations, the Holloways had been seafaring people – indeed, most in my branch of the family still are – and before purchasing the pub, head of the family Thomas senior had an impressive seafaring career behind him. As a young man he served aboard HMS *Ganges*, taking part in the 1794 Battle of Ushant where the British fleet managed to defeat the French despite sustaining major losses. Thomas met his future wife, Mary Chellew, a Cornish woman of comfortable financial means, and married in Falmouth in 1797. The marriage certificate lists Thomas as 'Mariner', which indicates that after leaving the Navy, he may well have been captain of his own vessel as a trader during the last years of the eighteenth century. The couple's first child arrived three years later, on 22 September 1800 – Thomas Holloway junior – born in the Robin Hood and Little John Inn at the end of a long, dry Cornish summer.

The first eleven years of Thomas junior's life were spent on the move. Thomas senior worked several jobs, and soon opened a baker's

shop in Falmouth whilst serving as a warrant officer in the local
militia – a combined local police force and home guard against the
very real threat of French invasion. The family moved several times
in Thomas junior's infancy, moving gradually further west, perhaps
to be closer to Mary's family, but the coastal links remained strong.
It must have felt natural to live by the sea amongst fishermen and
the soldiers returning from the war on the Continent.

Young Thomas, his parents, and siblings settled in Penzance
when he was eleven years old. Three more sisters were born over
the following decade: Caroline, Matilda and Emma. The expanding
Holloway family took over the oldest local inn, The Turk's Head,
watering hole to Navy ratings and gossiping locals. And there was
plenty to talk about. The Turk's Head had only just survived the
flames of the Spanish Armada, and the surrounding streets had
weathered centuries of pirate attacks, the plague, and even one
tsunami. The mansion at the end of the street was said to be
haunted by the ghost of its old resident, Mrs Baines, shot by her
own servant with a blunderbuss when she unwisely tried to test
his burglar-shooting skills. A priest was called in to perform an
exorcism on the house, and so the spirit of Mrs Baines moved on to
The Turk's Head to startle drinkers by materialising in her nightie
and bonnet. Most of the local mariners were more concerned with
earthly troubles. Every year, dozens of ships were wrecked on the
Cornish coast. Many locals drowned trying to save floating survivors
or loot the sinking brigs. For a child, the pub must have been a
thrilling place to play, with the cell in the courtyard for locking
up drunks and the narrow streets leading down to the harbour,
where the sea was known to offer up strange harvests of oranges
and port wine lost on their way to London.

Nevertheless, young Thomas's parents took his education
seriously, and he was assigned to a local tutor of some reputation,
John Spasshat, from a family of committed Baptists. It was an
odd choice for the Church of England Holloways, and considering
Thomas's later aversion for religion, it may not have been a happy

match. Nevertheless, we do know he was a bright child, a tenacious student, and good with languages. At the same time, Thomas and his brother Henry were no doubt expected to help their mother in the kitchen, and do the usual mopping and tankard collecting when the customers rolled in of an evening. Sending children to do these things was common practice at the time – a tipsy customer is more likely to tip a cheerful little boy than a tired landlord.

Pubs were bright centres of the community in the nineteenth century. Warmer and more inviting than the average tenement, it made sense for working men to spend their evenings amongst their friends, sharing stories and striking deals. For all his book learning with Spasshat, it was the pub where Thomas picked up the shrewdness he would later rely on in his role as the world-famous 'mighty healer'.

Accounts of Thomas's childhood are sparse. As an adult, Thomas wasn't prone to nostalgia. According to local legend, when the teenage Thomas finished his studies with Mr Spasshat, he took an apprenticeship at the local druggist's shop. There is little proof of this, but a fellow pupil of Spasshat's – Robert Hunt, whose time with the tutor overlapped Thomas's – went on to leave Penzance to open his own chemist and druggist shop. It is probable the boys knew each other and shared similar ambitions. Nevertheless, in a letter written forty years after entering the patent medicine trade, Thomas remembers his early experiments as a fledgling medicine man:

> I have, I believe, told you that the first ointment I made was in my mother's saucepan, which held about six quarts, an extra jump was in a long fish kettle and after that her little copper, which would hold an extra 40lb.

Quite what Mrs Holloway was expected to do about laundry and cooking while her son was clogging her copper with ointment, we don't know. But if Thomas was indeed apprentice to a local chemist as a lad, he would have been expected to do the repetitive chopping, boiling and rolling jobs for simple ointments and cosmetics; all easily replicated at home. It was hardly laboratory chemistry, but the local chemist and druggist's shop was the first stop for the average nineteenth-century family in need of quick and affordable treatment for everyday ailments. The druggists would mix up traditional poultices and pills to order, as well as patent medicines with secret ingredients – concoctions designed to keep customers from going to competitors. Thomas may well have fancied mixing his own concoctions, either out of curiosity or wishing to impress his masters.

Whatever truly happened, Thomas Holloway left Penzance and its limited opportunities at age twenty-eight. By 1828, the Napoleonic Wars were long over. His linguistic talents, along with his height and dark, sober looks, made him presentable enough to find work as a translator across the Channel. As a friend noted, Thomas had the look of a leader, something that aided business no end:

> In character he stood alone. Apart from his commanding stature (he stood well over 6 feet), in conversation he invariably impressed his hearers with the accuracy of judgement, to the extent that people were not only ready to follow his lead but were anxious to acquire information from him.

Compared to the Baptist chapels of Thomas's native Cornwall, post-war France was a novel scene where the order of things seemed completely reversed. Gambling, drink, fashion, and unpalatable food were all available at nearly half the expense of their English equivalents, making it the ideal destination for a young man looking to live cheaply and have plenty of fun. All manner of strange debauchery was open to anyone willing to try it. British guidebooks assured travellers that Dunkirk had no shortage of pubs happy to cater to young Englishmen, and good travel links to Paris, 'the most lively, the most dirty, the most noisy, but at the same time the most splendid and luxurious city in the world'. These guides preferred not to mention the knickerless girls dancing in the drinking dens and the city morgues displaying bodies for the public's grim amusement. Delicate warnings were directed towards the first-time traveller, lest they find themselves robbed by beautiful women targeting lone Englishmen, but Thomas flourished in Dunkirk. He and some bachelor friends formed the Société De l'Étoile in homage to the chivalric order of the 1300s. Together, they took rather un-knightly turns on the roulette wheels. Thomas looked back on this time of his youth with fondness.

Revelry wasn't the only way France differed to England. While the teenaged Thomas could mix up home remedies in his mother's kitchen and theoretically package and sell them himself, the French treated patent medicine with more suspicion. Though there was a place for small-time quacks in France, a licensing system put in place by the La Société Royale de Médecine after the 1780s had curtailed the sale of patent medicines. By the time Thomas visited France, local and national legislation had formally outlawed the sale of unlicensed medicine, making the kind of success an English quack might achieve almost impossible.

In England, such measures were considered impossible to enforce. More importantly, meddling in free trade was un-English, and the government were damned if they were going to take their lead from the French in anything. The physician Thomas Hodgkin hoped public taste would overwhelm the need for legislation. 'The public,' he wrote in 1830, 'may be so enlightened as to greatly diminish appetite' for patent medicines. Hodgkin was overly optimistic. Since the Restoration, quacks had been successfully forging royal seals of approval and inventing well-to-do patrons for the public to emulate. If legislation only encouraged more ingenuity, hoping for quackery's death by moral enlightenment was hopelessly naive. Quackery would always find a way.

Such a stark contrast may well have planted the seeds of ambition in Thomas's mind. Nevertheless, shortly after he returned to England,

Thomas's father died, leaving a small inheritance to his eldest son. Thomas was now the head of the family. Jaunts to France were no longer viable, and with Thomas senior's hard-working example hanging over him, he knew he had to knuckle down and find his profession. Thomas used his Continental contacts to establish his own importing company in London. His mother, brother Henry, and sister Mary Jane all came with him, setting up a new home in Cheapside before settling in the busy, commercial Broad Street in the City. Thomas spent his time acting as an interpreter at a hotel for a small income. It was here that he met the man who would change the course of his life: Felix Albinolo, professional quack.

A small man, darkly Italian, with a little English and a little French, Felix Albinolo had bold ambitions and a debatable past. Those who encountered him in his twilight years knew him as a lively figure, wandering Soho with a medal around his neck, claiming to have once led the French army to victory against the Prussians at Jena. In an article from *The Glasgow Herald* entitled 'A Very Strange Story', a journalist recounts how anyone who approached the elderly Albinolo would hear how:

> the battle was won, not by Bonaparte, but by Felix Albinolo! At a critical moment, Albinolo leapt out of the ranks, seizing a stray horse, and, riding in front of the soldiers, cried out, 'I am your Emperor, stand firm, all goes well, the battle is ours!' At this welcome news, the soldiers cheered with rapturous enthusiasm.

The likeness between the little Italian and Bonaparte was so great, the men rallied to his side and the Prussians were trounced. In leading the troops, Albinolo was gravely wounded. In the hospital bed he occupied for a year, he dreamed of his native Turin, where the women would mix poultices of mountain herbs completely unknown to the medical faculty to soothe the injuries of their families. Despite never again being healthy enough to step back into the French ranks, Albinolo claimed it was this folk remedy, mixed by his own hand – and with a little of his own added genius – that got him back on his feet when doctors thought all hope was lost.

Albinolo did well for himself amongst the Catholics of his native Turin with his 'St Come et St Damian Ointment'. He chose mystical imagery to lure his customers: snakes and all-seeing eyes floating alongside The Almighty himself, perched on a cloud. The allusion to the story of Saint Cosmo and Saint Damian was about as close as a man could get to offering a miracle in a jar. The story goes, Pope Felix IV was on the brink of death as a cancerous growth ate away at his thigh:

> And as he slept, the holy martyrs Cosmo and Damian appeared to him their devout servant, bringing with them an instrument and ointment of whom that one said to that other: Where shall we have flesh when we have cut away the rotten flesh to fill the void place? Then that other said to him: There is an Ethiopian that this day is buried in the churchyard of S. Peter ad Vincula, which is yet fresh, let us bear this thither, and take we out of that morian's flesh and fill this place withal. And so they fetched the thigh of the sick man and so changed that one for that other. And when the sick man awoke and felt no pain, he put forth his hand and felt his leg without hurt, and then took a candle, and saw well that it was not his thigh, but that it was another. And when he was well come to himself, he sprang out of his bed for joy.

According to legend, Saints Cosmo and Damian practised medicine without payment. Not so Albinolo. When profits permitted him to travel, he set his sights on England, where his marvelous ointment would range from 2s 9d to 33s, in addition to live leeches, wholesale and retail. When he arrived in London, Albinolo realised he needed an interpreter to help him craft enticing advertising copy for his product. In hiring Thomas Holloway, he had an ally who not only spoke the language, but one that looked respectable and possessed a knowledge of business to rival his own. The possibilities were exciting for both men. Did Thomas know what people would pay

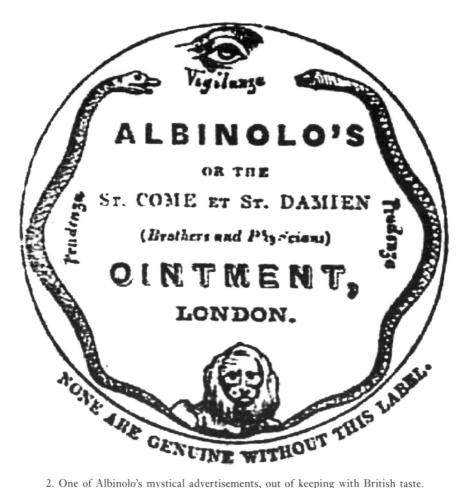

2. One of Albinolo's mystical advertisements, out of keeping with British taste.
(Verity Holloway)

for a simple folk remedy? Did he know what a young man with a bit of capital and nerve could make in this industry? Albinolo was a stranger in a foreign land, and he needed to get his foot in the door. Thomas knew England. He already had the wholesaling contacts. Together, they had a chance to do great things.

And they took it.

Chapter 2

To Quack Oneself

For Heaven's and for your own sakes,
Beware, my friends, beware of quacks ...
Think how egregiously they fool us,
Who vaunt, the same specific Bolus,
Or fam'd Elixir, can root out
A fever, dropsy, stone or gout! ...
Too sure I am, these boasted nostrums
Like those dispensed by country rostrums
More mortal men deprive of breath
Than Battle, Murder, Suddain Death.

Anonymous, *On the Prevailing Taste for*
Quack Medicine, c. 1766

To get a clearer picture of the business Thomas was about to embark on, let's first visit the Victorian medicine cabinet.

There was no National Health Service in Britain until the 1940s. A Victorian physician could make home visits to well-off patients, diagnose ailments, and prescribe treatments, but the medical professional as a whole was still ignorant of the origins of many diseases. A visit from the physician was prohibitively expensive to the majority of the public. More often than not, Victorians were forced to find their own remedies.

For centuries, apothecary shops were the destination for those seeking better health. In England, The Worshipful Society of Apothecaries was founded in 1617 with the motto *Opiferque Per Orbem Dicor* (Throughout the world I am called the bringer of help). The role of the apothecary was enshrined in livery long before this, with the Grocers' Company in 1345, and the Guild of Pepperers in 1180. Medieval accounts of English apothecary shops include macabre, charming details such as mummified crocodiles hanging from the walls. Interesting sights and smells were a major part of the business of selling health long before the nineteenth century. These shops would have their own proprietary medicines, made with closely guarded secret recipes sometimes written in code and bequeathed with pride to the next generation. These forerunners to patent medicines were known as nostrums, from the Latin 'ours'. As time went on, these nostrums continued to carry with them an air of exoticism and mystery, nodding to the medieval origins of the apothecary, when Christian physicians from Europe traded with the more advanced Eastern world. Expensive spices were imported to sell to intrigued English customers, promising miraculous properties no plant from home could rival.

By the end of the eighteenth century, the apothecary shop had split into two camps. The first was General Practitioners – plain dispensing chemists who dealt with physicians' prescriptions – and the second were 'trading' apothecaries, who, by the beginning of Queen Victoria's reign, had become known as the chemist and druggist. Here, the ordinary Victorian could approach the counter to complain about his runny nose, constipation or aching joints. Ingrowing toenails, bad teeth and small wounds could be dealt with by a surgeon barber, often the same man who cut your hair. This wasn't quite as haphazard as it sounds, though plenty of amateurs were known to try their luck. These surgeons honed their craft in long apprenticeships, and many only did so because the education required to become a physician was too expensive. Others simply invented qualifications and references, keeping on the move so as not to be caught.

The purchase of medicine was a chancy business. An ailing Victorian could turn to a number of places for medicinal advice and help, including booksellers, grocers, mail order catalogues, and locally-respected figures like the cunning women of old. None of these sources were entirely safe – regulation of medicinal substances and their vendors did not come until much later. Not unlike the high street pharmacy of today, the mid-Victorian chemist and druggist provided a dizzying array of products. From rat poison to homemade fragrances, a customer could stock up on all the necessary household chemicals, both related and unrelated to health and the body. Demand drove the chemist and druggist, and the staff needed the knowledge and ingenuity required to meet the needs of their customers. Powerful opiates and purgatives were sold alongside the traditional herbal remedies that remained in high demand after the Industrial Revolution. Take your ailment to the shop, and the staff would mix something up just for you.

Chemists and druggists were not required to hold dispensing qualifications. Although they were not strictly permitted to prescribe drugs the way a physician could, over-the-counter advice was the chemist and druggist's stock in trade. This, coupled with a lack of formal education, was a dangerous mix. As toxicologists like to quote Paracelsus: 'All things are poison and nothing is without poison; only the dose makes a thing not a poison.'

Laudanum addiction is a familiar story, louche and romantic as every Victorian tragedy should be. From Coleridge's drug-fuelled visionary poems to the Pre-Raphaelite artist and model Lizzie Siddal's death by overdose, many fell under the spell of this elixir of alcohol and opium. But for every high profile tragedy, there are countless other incidences of addiction, infant mortality, suicide and accidental death. For menstrual pain, toothache or nervousness, a few drops of laudanum were a godsend for people from all over the social spectrum, and it was easily procurable. For the working classes especially, accidents came about by simply trying to make a living. Without access to reliable contraception, a woman with several children would still need to work, necessitating her to put her babies to sleep while she was out and quieting them while she tried to rest. Opiate addiction takes away the appetite, causing babies to quietly waste away. The *Punch* cartoon overleaf shows

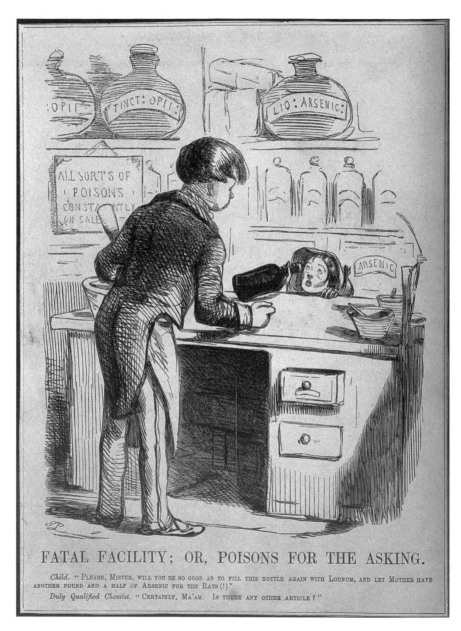

3. *Punch* cartoon depicting an unscrupulous chemist selling a child arsenic and laudanum.
Wood engraving after J. Leech.
(Wellcome Library, London)

a small child being sent to top up her mother's laudanum bottle at the chemist and druggist's, along with the family supply of arsenic. Procuration of poisons was laughably simple, and here *Punch* alludes to the custom of sending a child to the pub to fetch the dinner beer. Children were accustomed to the presence of dangerous substances, and such casual proximity had inevitable consequences.

Arsenic was another staple of the chemist and druggist's shop. A death from arsenic poisoning is a terrible thing to behold, with 'agonies that would soften the heart of a savage'. With one sufficient dose, the victim would exhibit grotesque salivation, abdominal pain, vomiting, bloody diarrhoea, seizures and even exterior skin burns before coma and death. Slow arsenic poisoning from frequent small doses could bring about jaundice, hair loss, muscle wasting and gangrene, before an equally fatal conclusion. As powdered arsenic was a common household item, tasteless, and similar in appearance to sugar, it was sometimes impossible to tell a murder from an accident. This made it the weapon of choice for women who wanted rid of their husbands, leading to a wave of poison panics in the mid-nineteenth century, and a number of high-profile executions on dubious grounds. As many at the time argued, if a nineteenth-century housewife could be hanged for possessing a deadly substance, there would be no housewives left.

This popular terror did not, however, stop arsenic from being marketed as a beauty product and sometimes even an aphrodisiac. Within Britain's clandestine transvestite community, diluted arsenic was employed to remove body hair. Being a method of preserving perishables, arsenic became known as a preserver of fine complexions. Arsenic wafers (tablets) promised women skin 'free from any spot or blemish whatsoever', while men turned to arsenic washes as a cure for baldness. One particularly dangerous myth attached to the poison was that of 'the arsenic eaters of Austria', who, it was said, attributed their ethereal beauty to daily doses of the poison. If they were to stop for one day, they claimed, their faces would wither within hours. Despite these patent tablets and soaps containing little to no arsenic, deaths still occurred as the toxin built up inside the bloodstream. Tragically, knowing their beautifying toiletries contained so little of the magic substance, some women took to scraping arsenic off fly paper to make their own, stronger versions, believing them to be superior.

Other poisons, too, had common medicinal purposes, and were easily procurable from the local chemist and druggist's. Strychnine was sometimes prescribed for lethargy or depression, or used by unscrupulous brewers to bulk up beer. Take too much, and the

4. Nineteenth-century pharmaceutical bottles.
(Verity Holloway)

patient could find their muscles locking into place and sweat sticking their clothes to their bodies. If they were lucky, they would not go on to die of asphyxiation as the body exhausted itself with violent contractions. Deadly nightshade was recommended as a paste to be applied directly to the breasts to stop the flow of milk, and was famously used to add alluring sparkle to women's eyes. Mercury was not the reserve of the philandering male. Jane Austen's 7-year-old niece was prescribed mercury to draw water off the brain, and it was also applied to ease pain in swollen joints. Everyday cough mixtures and teething soothers contained strong emetics (vomit inducers), risking side effects far worse than the ailment itself.

One would hope such dangerous substances were dispensed at the discretion of qualified physicians. A glance at the domestic medicine chest of the average middle-class home shows the opposite. Attractive wooden chests were sold to housewives, stocked with all the chemicals a woman needed to care for her family. On top of equipment for DIY bleeding, the chests contained powerful poisons, laxatives, emetics and first aid manuals on how to resuscitate after poisoning and drowning. From the 1760s to the 1890s, twenty such manuals were published and sold alongside well-stocked medicine chests for the home, and went through many editions. These books recommended first consulting a physician in all cases, but as Mrs Beeton's wildly popular household guides attest, a good housewife was self-reliant in all things, including dosing up the family. Beeton's 1859 advice on home care for strokes reads like an assault:

> Place in bed with head raised. Bleed freely at once from the arm. Apply warm mustard poultices to the soles of feet and inside of thighs. Administer two drops of castor oil and 8 grains of calomel. Administer a turpentine enema. Cut off the hair and apply rags soaked in vinegar to the head. If the blood vessels of the head and neck are much swollen apply eight to ten leeches to the temple opposite the side that is paralysed.

This culture of self-reliance provided the perfect climate for a thriving alternative medicine scene. The nineteenth century was a golden age of pseudoscience, when preposterous inventions made fortunes out of the public's curiosity, fashion-consciousness, or plain desperation. Phrenology – the 'science' of inspecting the skull for bumps that correspond with psychological traits – gained popularity after Queen Victoria sent her children to 'have their bumps read'. According to one London bump-reader, the poetic genius of Keats was undeniably the product of scrofula on the brain, much to the amusement of the local students who visited him for a laugh. Though a novelty to most people, phrenology was a lucrative business. Chiropodists, too, offered questionable services. An enterprising chiropodist could remove phantom corns buried deep inside the foot by massaging the healthy appendage and producing bits of dried leather from a handkerchief for the patient to inspect with disgust. When you could charge per corn, chiropody was a wise career choice, providing you had the gall for it and could tolerate the smell.

However, phrenology and chiropody required the patient to visit a specialist. Mail order medicine was a far more effective method of making money. The discovery of electricity led to a barrage of electric tonics and accessories, promising to energise and strengthen the body. Mr C.B. Harness took out large newspaper advertisements for his Electropathic Battery Belt, which was 'an invaluable health appliance for the treatment and cure of disease'. Delightfully comfortable to wear, the belt, which came in male and female styles (the female being exactly the same as the male, save for a pretty bow on the front), were 'an inestimable blessing to suffering humanity in all parts of the world'. That is to say, completely useless. Harness's ads promised 'health without physic', meaning potentially harmful medicines. Awareness of the risks associated with visiting a qualified physician meant the public demand for alternative medicine was high.

5. Harness's Electropathic Belt promised to cure frailty with the power of magnetism.
(Verity Holloway)

Throughout the entire nineteenth century, the craze for old-fashioned nostrums lived alongside modern fads like the Electropathic Belt. The attitude that the traditional and the modern, the alternative and the scientific, were at odds with one another is a more modern attitude. Patients in the eighteenth and nineteenth centuries were practically expected to experiment in the search for a cure, sometimes mixing a physician's advice with that of numerous quacks. The same patient could happily visit a newfangled mesmerist in the morning for a spot of animal magnetism, and a urine doctor after lunch. These urine doctors, affectionately known as piss prophets, pedalled a diagnostic method harking back to the middle ages. Setting up shop all over towns and cities, piss prophets promised to diagnose any illness through the colour of urine alone. They could even do it by post. The fact that some of these piss prophets were unmasked as qualified physicians moonlighting for extra cash goes to show how much money was in quackery.

While fads came and went, ointments and pills dominated the alternative medicine market. Nowadays, the phrase 'patent medicine' conjures a circus sideshow scene with a salesman hawking wares from a caravan. This is one aspect of quackery, but far from the whole picture. Certainly, on the streets of English cities, the salesman hawking bottles from a basket was a familiar enough sight for it to be satirised in political cartoons and religious pamphlets. One could purchase homebrewed cough mixtures, laxatives, and dozens of other daily remedies without ever having to step inside the chemist and druggist's door. This habit of parading the streets, calling out, may have been where the phrase 'quack' originates, shortened from the Dutch 'quacksalver', meaning a hawker of salves. To 'quack oneself' was to dose up on these remedies. There were mountebanks, too, who literally mounted barrows and chairs to gain attention, and charlatans, from the Italian *chiarlare*, meaning to chatter. In a marketplace scenario, this would have been a familiar way of doing business, and these quacks were known to employ theatrical elements to stand out from their competitors. Cartoons show quacks in bright costumes accompanied by chained monkeys or snakes. Mountebanks could ply their trade over a whole town from the back of a horse-drawn carriage – drive-by quackery. One coloured etching from 1817 depicts a nightmarish scene in which a foppish quack practises dentistry on a victim held down by a laughing clown. An audience crowds around the stage, fascinated and repulsed.

That is an extreme example. For centuries, simple homemade remedies were a staple of everyday life in England, with lone women catering to the needs of small villages, midwifing and mixing poultices, often for free. A mixture of religious counselling and grandmotherly comfort made these cheap alternatives to the apothecary or physician popular and trustworthy. In time, legitimate physicians would force many of these people to the sidelines, but the demand for individuals touting homemade remedies, no matter how dubious, never went away.

So what precisely is a quack doctor? What sets him or her aside from eighteenth and nineteenth-century physicians simply working with the limited knowledge they had, which was often erroneous?

Firstly, a quack was always someone else. It didn't matter if you were a practising physician with an expensive degree, a grandmother whisking up a family remedy, or a charlatan selling pills at the summer fair   by branding someone else a quack, you took attention away from your own mistakes or dubious practices, and you set yourself aside from the rabble. Quack doctors were always quick and happy to brand their competitors as such. No one referred to themselves as a quack. It is purely a derogatory term. Despite their diverse tactics, their patter, and their trademark tricks, one thing all quacks had in common was their insistence that they weren't one of the bad guys.

For the purpose of this book, a quack is someone who knowingly deceives the public with a self-concocted, usually 'secret' remedy of little or no medical value. At best, these nostrums were useless. At worst, they could kill. Some Victorian quack companies still exist

6. An Italian quack, or 'chialare', hawking his wares. Oil painting, Anon.
(Wellcome Library, London)

today in name only, having stepped into the world of legitimate medicine to become familiar household names. Others are so shameless it's hard to believe they ever existed.

It's understandable that Victorian consumers had what appears now to be a cavalier attitude to medicine, but we cannot underestimate the power of desperation. When faced with a terminal illness, it's little wonder patients would search frantically for a miracle cure. And there was no shortage of entrepreneurial types happy to use this desperation to their advantage.

It is difficult to write about quacks without projecting a modern-day moral judgement. But such an outlook rather detracts from the quack doctor's undeniable magnetism, and his endurance through the centuries. It doesn't take a giant leap of imagination to draw parallels between today's homeopathy, miracle diets and unpronounceable herbal supplements, and the travelling salesmen of centuries past, promising salvation in return for lightening your purse. There have always been quacks because there has always been a demand for them.

The epithet of quack carries with it a whiff of class snobbery. In eighteenth-century England, intellectuals bemoaned the dumbing down of society thanks to swiftly changing fashions, trash literature and the popularity of cheap patent medicines. It naturally followed that quack doctors accused the educated classes of sneering at their fellow men – something *they*, with their public-spirited enterprises, would never do. Quacks knew the arguments of their enemies and were adept at turning them into advantages. There were quacks who protested that their advertising to the lower social strata came from a desire to improve the lives of their fellow men. Only a very condescending fellow would call that fishing for suckers. Some of these quacks even held respectable medical degrees, much to the annoyance of qualified doctors. Instead of catering to the needs of families, they chose to pitch themselves at a working-class crowd with flashy salesmanship and more than a dash of theatre. It was practically a prostitution of the healing art, medical men said, seeing no irony in keeping their doors closed to the poor. A little knowledge of conventional medicine was another weapon in the quack's arsenal, frightening potential customers with a grain of truth about the gory reality of nineteenth-century surgery. Many miracle cures specifically promised to save the sick from 'the knife'.

In the search of a cure, a consumer had to rely on his or her wits. It didn't help that legitimate doctors and quacks could be cursed in the same breath. As early as 1710, the *Tory Tatler* summed up the plight of the sick:

Distempers seize Men, but the Physicians execute 'em. For my part, I never hear an Apothecary's Mortar ringing, but I think the

Bell's a tolling; nor read a Doctor's Prescription, but I take it for a Passport into the next World.

Given the choice between the expensive experience of blood-letting, blistering, and purges, and an easily taken pill promising instant relief, it's easy to see why legitimate physicians were viewed with suspicion. To make matters worse, the physicians of the nineteenth century were notoriously lacking in bedside manner, whereas quacks knew how to sympathise. A telling example of this is the success of Poor Man's Friend ointment for fistulas, wounds, and bruises. Formulated in 1790s Dorset, Poor Man's Friend was so popular, it was still available to purchase nearly 200 years later. Beautifully illustrated adverts depicted salesmen coming out of the country darkness to the rescue of virtuous beggars, promising health 'without confinement or change of diet', both of which were too expensive to contemplate. Quacks captured the imaginations of their customers. Once a customer felt emotionally understood, money was much more likely to change hands. But, as the 1845 cartoon overleaf attests, for all the promises of patent medicines and their gushing testimonials, it was undeniably the poor who were being exploited. Poor Man's Friend contained lead and mercury.

By the beginning of the nineteenth century, print media had blossomed sufficiently to give creators of patent medicines a national platform without the necessity of travel. Flick though any daily paper and one would find men of the cloth promising to share their secret to a full head of hair at sixty. Married women would post advertisements offering an end to the drinking habits of bad husbands. For a fee, naturally. There was little to no way of knowing which, if any, of these column inches was genuine and which were cottage industries set up to prey on people's insecurities. From corns to cancer, if an ailment had a name, there was an unscrupulous character happy to do whatever it took to make money from it. Popular cartoons depicted quacks as villains, either monstrously grotesque or lecherously handsome. But to a casual reader, these

THE POOR MAN'S FRIEND.

7. One of countless *Punch* cartoons decrying patent medicine as a tax on the gullibility and desperation of the poor. Note the testimonial on the wall. Published 1845.
(Wellcome Library, London)

advertisements were comforting and familiar; perhaps even the
answer to their prayers.

> Mister Baxter of Leeds, lately Hull, has restored sight to many
> hundreds of individuals, many of whom have been blind for five,
> ten, fifteen, twenty, and forty-five years ... without blisters, bleeding,
> issues, or any restraint of diet.
>
> *The Northern Star*, 4 May 1830

> Dr Taylor's highly esteemed ANTI-SPASMODIC PILLS, a late
> discovery of a medical gentleman of great eminence, being the
> only specific cure of Epilepsy, or Falling Sickness, Convulsion Fits,
> Hysteric and Paralytic Affections, Cramp in the Stomach, and an
> antidote of that mortal malady, the Apoplexy.
>
> *Hull Packet*, Tuesday, 15 May 1810

> Henry's Magic Pills, for the cure of the gout, rheumatic gout,
> rheumatism, and all rheumatic affections. It contains neither mercury,
> antimony, nor any other kind of noxious substance; relieves a fit
> of the gout or rheumatism in any hour or two; gives soothing and
> refreshing sleep; and in many cases, I have known patients walk
> well and easy in less than twenty-four hours.
>
> *Birmingham Journal*, Saturday, 25 March 1843

Of course, it's unfair to imagine a nineteenth-century reader
falling for anything and everything they read. Some scams are
more obvious than others, and as time went on, successful patent
medicine companies chose to commit to the flashy route, or a path
of face-value respectability. It follows that not all patent medicines
were aimed at the hoi polloi. Indeed, the expanding urban, literate
classes had access to a wealth of print media, bookshops and
circulating libraries, and since the Georgian era, this demographic
offered rich pickings to the nostrum vendor. The railways, too,
made the lives of mountebanks much easier, allowing an energetic
individual to visit several towns a day where once he would have
been confined to his local patch. Conversely, he could get out of

town quickly if need be. If you did especially well, you could set up shop, advertise widely, and wait for the punters to come to you.

For us to better understand the business Thomas Holloway and Felix Albinolo were embarking upon, let's take a look at the careers of a few notable quacks.

Chapter 3

Rogue's Gallery

I hereby certify and swear to it, that at the age of fifteen years I had the misfortune to fall into the crater of Vesuvius, and was burned to a cinder; but on taking two of Parr's Life Pills, I completely recovered.
The Anatomy of Quackery, 1853

In the world of nineteenth-century patent medicine, truth was the first casualty of war. The second was modesty.

8. Doctor Humbugallo, an itinerant medicine vendor, selling his wares from a stage with an assistant dressed as a court fool. Watercolour by T. Rowlandson. Early nineteenth century.
(Wellcome Library, London)

'The Knife Superseded'

In the case of Burgess's Lion Ointment, first on the market in 1847, if you were going to put your name to a product, that product had to be utterly superlative. Avoiding a horrifying amputation was a priority for most Victorians, and Edwin Burgess, a former south London hairdresser, decided his ointment was a viable alternative.

> Cure the worst and most obstinate cases of Ulcers, Abcesses, Cancers, Tumours, Polypi, Carbuncles, Piles, poisoned wounds of all kinds (including Dog and Venomous Bites) and every form of Eruption and Skin Disease; also Ulcerated and Cancerous Affections peculiar to Females, without the aid of Lancet or Knife. Numbers have been cured after leaving various London Hospitals as incurable, or curable only by amputation.

Take two pills before bedtime and apply the ointment as necessary. The formula would then draw the disease from its source and filter the blood, purifying it with miraculous efficacy.

One testimonial, printed in *The Chemist & Druggist*, read:

> Dear Sir,
> I am happy to forward to you the following testimonial of the great value of your Lion Ointment and Pills. Through the ill-treatment of my husband, I have been suffering with poisoned blood, and, in consequence, a large abscess in my neck, also syphilis affecting my leg. I consulted several physicians who said I should not recover unless I had the bone taken out. I was advised to use your Lion Ointment and Pills, and I am happy to say they saved my life and I am now perfectly cured. Hoping through my case your wonderful Ointment and Pills may get well known for the benefit of my poor fellow creatures.
> I am, sir, yours respectfully, Miss Elizabeth Stillwell

Top marks to whoever came up with that surname. The useful thing about syphilis is that the telltale abscesses have a way of disappearing as the disease progresses to its more serious stages, making the patient momentarily believe their suffering is over.

An investigation by the British Medical Association found that Burgess's miraculous pills were little more than minty laxatives: 'Chemical and microscopical examination indicated the presence of ipecacuanha, rhubarb, a little jalap, probably aloes (Socotrine), and oil of peppermint, and soap. There was no evidence of the presence of mercury or calomel.'

The good news was that Burgess's Lion Ointment and Pills wouldn't poison you. The bad news was that you might need that amputation after all. The ointment is still manufactured in Hebden Bridge today, with a modified recipe to make it easier to absorb into the skin. All claims of extraordinary healing powers have long since gone. Nowadays, Burgess's Ointment is restricted to treating minor skin problems. Ernest Burgess himself died of 'softening of the brain', leaving the business to his son, who continued to market this cheap alternative to the knife.

'So easy and innocent'

One of the longest-surviving patent medicines was Anderson's Scots Pills, or Grana Angelica (Angel's Grains). Once claiming to be the physician to Charles I, Scottish physician Patrick Anderson is said to have come across the recipe for his acclaimed pills in 1630s Venice, where traders came together from all corners of the globe. The secret recipe was passed down through Anderson's family and that of his successor, Dr Weir. The fall of the monarchy put paid to Anderson's hard-won royal patent, and by the time Weir took out his own patent (which would soon be overturned by Parliament), piracy had broken out and was never fully quashed. Several individuals claimed to have the one true recipe, though the nature of the game of quackery meant never to let on what that recipe actually involved. One chancer – a Mister Man –

distributed boxes of Scots Pills at his local coffee house; cheerful counterfeit boxes bearing the legend 'remember you must die'. Of the many to profit from Anderson's 'secret' recipe, Miss Isabella Inglish arguably did the best in the early 1700s, proclaiming in a pamphlet that she had royal dispensation to make and distribute the pills, having been given the recipe by Dr Weir while working as his servant. More likely, she pinched it, but this didn't stop her putting her own name to the pills in the form of an ornate wax seal.

So what did Anderson's Scots Pills do that made them so sought after? The original formula was said to contain over forty different ingredients and took about four days to produce by boiling, straining and rolling into pill form. By 1824, analysis of Anderson's Scots Pills told a different story: Barbados aloes, soap, colocynth, gamboge, and aniseed oil. Essentially a laxative, myrrh was later added to the mixture for a stimulant effect. Arguably, if a customer wanted a gentle purgative pick-me-up, he would be better off visiting Mister Man's coffee house. However, Anderson's Scots Pills had a list of twelve curative properties set down soberly enough to make them seem trustworthy:

> They comfort the bowels and remove all obstructions in these parts ... They strengthen the Head and Senses ... They are beneficial to all Diseases of Women ... They kill all kind of Worms ... They defend the body against Surfeit in Eating and Drinking, which frequently beget crude Humours.

Seasickness, brain fog, migraines, gout, palsy – Anderson's Scots Pills were 'of so easy and innocent operation, they may be given to a child or very old person'. The pills were wildly successful, but being so easily counterfeited, it was inevitable that the brand eventually faded away at the end of the nineteenth century. Still, the longevity was impressive, considering Miss Inglish took out an ad in *The Observator* in 1708, complaining of one 'Mussen, who sells a notorious Counterfeit, instead of the true Pill, within three Doors of me'.

Baby Killers

The rate of child mortality in the nineteenth century continues to be debated. The usual quoted statistic is that one in five children didn't make it to their fifth birthday, but, as many historians have pointed out, this isn't based on empirical evidence and doesn't take into account the differences in city and country dwellings, or class. Certainly, the loss of a child was a far more common tragedy than it is today. The first few years of an infant's life were considered the most precarious, with teething as a major source of discomfort and infection. As teething and its related problems was considered as a risk factor leading to chronic disabilities like epilepsy and deafness, countless products were offered to ease the anxious mother through this difficult period. In 1911, the American Medical Association put out a publication called 'Articles on the nostrum evil and quackery'. Under an illustration of a skeletal hand clutching bottles of infant anodynes, Mrs Winslow's Soothing Syrup is named in four separate cases of infant death in as many years. The chapter heading reads, 'Baby Killers'.

Mrs Winslow's Soothing Syrup first appeared in the 1830s, accredited to a nurse who had thirty years of pediatric experience under her belt. Marketed in Britain and America, the syrup was taken off the shelves in the 1940s. A brand leader for much of that time, the syrup was one of the nineteenth century's most widely advertised products, making use of newspapers and periodicals, as well as collectable trade cards, posters, family recipe books and celebrity endorsements. Many of these ads are undeniably gorgeous, drawing on Victorian fantasies of the ideal nuclear family where the mother reigns over the home like a serene queen. Babies smile, surrounded by their cherubic siblings, and mothers haven't a care in the world.

Depend on it, Mothers, it will give rest to yourselves and RELIEF
& HEALTH TO YOUR INFANTS.

Another advert aims to drive away the doubts of the cautiously
sceptical mother:

If you have a Suffering Child, do not let your prejudices, or the
prejudices of others, stand between it and the relief that will be
absolutely sure to follow the use of MRS WINSLOW'S SOOTHING
SYRUP. It has been used for over fifty years by millions of mothers
for their children with perfect safety and success.

And worst of all:

No family should be without a bottle of MRS WINSLOW'S
SOOTHING SYRUP in the house. The numerous deaths among
children might be avoided by its timely use.

Regardless of any nursing credentials Mrs Winslow truly possessed
– if she existed at all – her syrup was indeed a baby killer. Of
course, the initial effects seemed like a godsend. Fussy babies fell
asleep and diarrhoea was quelled. But with a base of opium and
alcohol, mothers dosing their children risked infant addiction,
coma and death. By the 1870s, when the instances of deaths were
too numerous to sweep under the carpet, the manufacturers were
keen to say the syrup contained no opium at all – merely aniseed.
It was only in the early twentieth century that the packaging
finally confessed to small quantities of morphine, 'along with
other valuable ingredients'. In 1909, opiates were removed from
the British version of the product altogether. It still contained
alcohol.

Try as the medical establishment might, they couldn't stamp
out the immense public appeal of patent medicines. Their alluring
advertising and affordable prices, coupled with the popular view
of hospitals as somewhere one went to die, patent medicines

were a staggering money spinner ground deep into the public's consciousness. Without proper regulation of ingredients or advertising promises, healing oneself in the mid-nineteenth century was a risky business, courting deception and death. Making money, however, was easy.

Chapter 4

Crafting the Professor

As sickness is the usual forerunner of death, it should therefore lead you seriously to consider, and reflect on your behaviour in life, and carefully to examine yourselves how far you are prepared for that great change.
From 'Directions and prayers for the use of the Patients', by the Chaplain of St Thomas's Hospital, c. 1819

Such was the state of alternative medicine when Thomas Holloway met Felix Albinolo. At first, the Italian simply needed an interpreter, and Thomas was glad to oblige. His importing business was only just supporting his family, who had come to live with him in London, and his eldest sisters showed no sign of marrying to lighten the burden. With his St Come et St Damien Ointment, Albinolo was seemingly ignorant of British anti-Catholic sentiment. Thomas helped rid Albinolo's advertisements of saints and papal legends, bringing it up to date as 'one of the greatest discoveries of this century for the welfare of humanity'. The ointment promised salvation to almost everyone:

For the cure of Cancer, Scrofula, Eruptions of the Skin, Contagious Diseases, Cholera, Plague, Wounds, Burns, Pains or Aches of any kind, Lues [an archaic term for syphilis, pronounced 'Louise'], Sea Sickness, and various other Diseases.

Thomas knew that to thrive, the Italian needed a patron, preferably a medical man, to endorse his products. Testimonials were easy to forge, and patent medicine manufacturers were notorious for inventing medical characters to add credibility their products, often with meaningless but impressive looking collections of letters after their name. However, if one wished to establish oneself as a trustworthy healer, an encouraging note from a flesh-and-blood physician was invaluable. Thomas introduced Albinolo to the staff of St Thomas's Hospital, on the site of a twelfth-century Augustinian infirmary in Southwark. St Thomas's had long been known as an establishment particularly partial to gifts of cash, which may suggest Holloway intended to pay the hospital for a testimonial and perhaps offer a crate of ointment for the wards. This reputation, plus eighteenth-century stories of patients running away (either to escape cruel treatments or visit the adjoining gin shops) had given St Thomas's a bad name. By the time Thomas and Albinolo made their visit, major renovations had taken place, architecturally and morally, and the pair were promptly told their miraculous ointment was no different to any other patent product already in use at the hospital. Maybe Thomas had led his new partner to expect a more favourable outcome, but after St Thomas's, the Holloway-Albinolo relationship began to disintegrate.

One of two things happened. Either Thomas realised that because all patent ointments were essentially the same he could easily set up alone, or he simply decided the problem with Albinolo's business was Albinolo himself. Either way, the pair fell out, and hugely. What followed was an episode they would both live to bitterly regret – and one that would make Thomas Holloway's name.

The product was easy enough to make alone. Albinolo had been all too happy to distribute his ointment recipe to interested parties. Perhaps he did so to Thomas, neglecting to protect himself beforehand, but nevertheless, the miraculous grease contained simple butter, salt and wax, along with a handful of proprietary ingredients with mystical names alluding to snakes – all of which were little but vegetable matter. Experimenting with leftover kitchen grease and oils as he had in Penzance, Thomas was able to create a colourless ointment easily absorbed into the skin. The smell left something to be desired, but adding cheap spices helped, playing on the lingering cultural memory of the apothecary shop with its exotic imported wares.

For distribution, Thomas started small, with the crowd he knew. He met the fleet as they docked, offering free samples to sailors. Sickness amongst sailors was a serious concern in the 1830s, when Thomas first tried his luck. Aside from all the usual bugs and venereal diseases, sailors carried far more serious contagions from the tropics and the Black Sea. The cholera outbreak of 1831 was likely brought to English shores by sailors, and in the following decades, it was alarmingly common for ships to return to port with half their crew dead, owing to yellow fever or other diseases. The situation was not helped by the Navy's unwillingness to quarantine the sick. The British Empire relied on its trade routes. If every ship carrying a mysteriously sick sailor was dealt with in a sensible manner, money would be lost, not to mention the potential for riots when a crew realised they were locked in with death. Prophylactics such as quinine were embraced by the Navy and their healing properties exaggerated, not least because they encouraged men to enlist who otherwise would have been put off by the dangers of the tropics. Free samples of patent medicines were unlikely to be discouraged.

But word of mouth, sailor-to-sailor, did little to conjure the business Thomas needed to move his operation out of his kitchen. Attempting door-to-door sales with a basket of ointment bore little fruit either, though housewives later recalled the tall Cornishman as unusually courteous and soft-spoken for a travelling quack. He was not a natural speaker or showman. His brother Henry seems to have inherited the gift of the gab, and would be useful to Thomas later, but for now, Thomas needed to market his wares in print. And for that, he needed to re-evaluate himself.

For anyone taking a walk down a city street in the nineteenth century, the sheer quantity of advertising was an assault on the eyes: posters pasted over posters, as high as a ladder could reach, on every available wall. *Punch* joked that the sight of countless advertisements was like a poor man's Royal Academy exhibition; a grotesque artistic counter-culture. Fonts warred with each other, exclamation marks bawled, and cartoons and puns of varying quality tried to catch and hold the eye of the literate and illiterate alike.

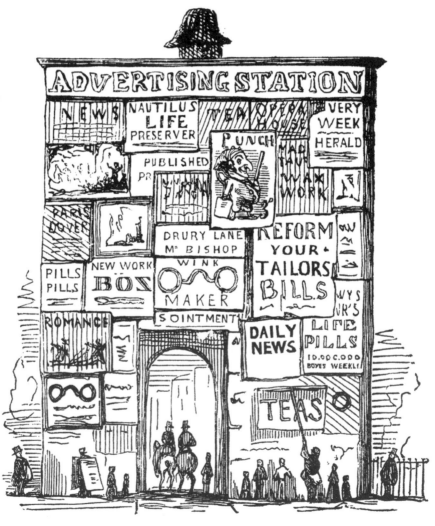

9. An 1846 *Punch* cartoon satirising the posters choking every available wall in London.
(Verity Holloway)

Charles Dickens, in an 1851 edition of his weekly magazine *Household Words*, penned a comic piece on bill stickers after coming across a London house suffocated by advertising:

> It would have been impossible to say, on the most conscientious survey, how much of its front was brick and mortar, and how much decaying and decayed plaster. It was so thickly encrusted with fragments of bills, that no ship's keel after a long voyage could be half so foul. All traces of the broken windows were billed out, the doors were billed across, the water-spout was billed over. The building was shored up to prevent its tumbling in to the street; and the very beams erected against it, were less wood than paste and paper, they had been so continually posted and reposted. The forlorn dregs of old posters so encumbered this wreck, that there was no hold for new posters, and the stickers had abandoned the place in despair.

Amongst the playbills, cocoa advertisements and casual jobs, a wanderer through mid-Victorian London would have been hard-pressed not to notice the promises of Thomas Holloway's celebrated pills and ointments. Long after Thomas's partnership with Albinolo came to an end, Dickens certainly noticed:

> If I had an enemy whom I hated – which Heaven forbid! – and if I knew of something that sat heavy on his conscience, I think I would introduce that something into a Posting Bill, and place a large impression in the hands of an active sticker. I can scarcely imagine a more terrible revenge. I should haunt him, by this means, night and day. ... Has any man a self-reproachful thought associated with pills, or ointment? What an avenging spirit to that man is PROFESSOR HOLLOWAY!

Advertising, properly harnessed, was a force to be reckoned with, and Thomas Holloway knew it. For Thomas's grandparents' generation, face-to-face transactions were the only transactions, but those days were fast becoming history. In times past, one could inspect the goods, assess the likeability and trustworthiness of the vendor, and make an informed decision based on local opinion. Print ads offered no such security, and there are countless accounts of early nineteenth-century customers dismayed to find themselves paying for shoddy merchandise after reading fulsome promises. There was little legislation in place to stop a businessman outright lying in his advertisements. It wasn't unknown for the word 'magic' to crop up, and an element of the circus sideshow was ever-present, with advertisements taking on the tone of a funfair announcer warming up the crowd. Repeated slogans yell at the reader in bold fonts with hysterical punctuation. One hair growth serum asked men, 'Do you want a moustache? Do you want a moustache?? Do you want a moustache???', whilst a speech therapist used her inch of print space in *The Illustrated London News* to insist, 'EVERY STUTTERER can read. EVERY STUTTERER should read. EVERY STUTTERER must read. EVERY STUTTERER may read.' Even with our relentless modern twenty-four-hour advertising, reading the advertising pages of the average Victorian newspaper is mentally exhausting. Sections of text are tightly packed, mainly sans illustrations, often with only thin lines separating them from their neighbours, and words are squintingly small. When you scan a Victorian newspaper, it quickly becomes apparent that standing out was key.

Albinolo stood out, but for all the wrong reasons. Whatever Thomas's true motivations were in breaking away from Albinolo, the question of image certainly looms large. In early Victorian Britain, the nation's many Italian immigrants were an attractive relic of the Romantic age when a Grand Tour of Italy was a cultural must for the wealthier classes. However, Italian was falling out of fashion as a second language for British students, replaced by Prince Albert's German, and an unpleasant stereotype of sneakiness was rising to the surface of the average Englishman's consciousness. You would buy a penny lick of ice cream from an Italian, but lifesaving medication was another matter entirely, particularly when, like Albinolo's miraculous ointment, 'popish superstition' was part of the package. In the world of patent medicine, exoticism was a tried-and-tested way to grab attention, but any benefit to be had by Latin mystique had to be weighed against prevailing stereotypes of Italians as lazy and sly. One such notable rogue had already been and gone – the flamboyant Baron Spolasco. Real name, as unlikely as it sounds: John Smith.

Adopting a Mediterranean name, blackened hair and a touch of rouge, Baron Spolasco was in fact English. A self-proclaimed physician and surgeon, Spolasco took a Latin persona and roamed Britain, leaving illegitimate children almost everywhere he went. His aim was to spread his healing genius, which consisted of two strong laxatives and a stiff drink for each patient, no matter the ailment. Spolasco is one of those nineteenth-century rogues one can't help but admire for sheer gall. Indicted for manslaughter after one of his pills perforated the stomach of a young woman, Spolasco wrote poetry extolling his own virtues and charged the wealthy a guinea simply to see him.

> *I pledge unto SPOLASCO'S name*
> *A name in which we glory*
> *His splendid CURES and HEALING fame*
> *Recorded are in story.*

The 'singularly talented' Baron's list of curable complaints included leprosy, cancer, epilepsy, all kinds of venereal disease, freckles, smallpox, and corns. He eventually shortened this list to 'every disease known to us'. Not one to limit his repertoire, the Baron occasionally turned his hand to rhinoplasty for those who had lost their noses to syphilis, offering a range of shapes and sizes to suit all faces. After one such operation, the Baron commented with surprise that the patient bled profusely when the flap of skin was lifted from his forehead and sewn to his face.

Parading around in a splendid coach with a black manservant in uniform and cockades, Spolasco was run out of town on more than one occasion. The people of London, in particular, did not warm to his charm. They had seen it all before. A flashy foreign name and a dash of glamour could easily work against a businessman wanting to break into that most lucrative market – the British nuclear family. Fleeing to America in his old age, where exoticism was still a boon to the quack, critics continued to write about the Baron in terms of comedic value; how he unconvincingly dyed his hair black and carried himself like an aging European roué. By his death in the 1850s, Spolasco was referred to in the press as an outright quack who 'wore a mountebank costume' – the centuries-old shorthand for a fraud. This sort of Latin theatricality might work in the short term, but if a man wanted a lasting business, he needed to think more strategically. Thomas Holloway knew all trace of Albinolo and his tall tales of Napoleonic swashbuckling had to be erased.

It wasn't enough to pedal an ointment. One needed a character. Holloway's Ointment needed a ramrod of stability behind it, and while other patent medicines relied on fictional reverends and barons as their figurehead, Thomas decided to run with 'Professor'. The title was just vague enough not to be an outright lie – after all, he was 'professing' his brilliance – and with his impressive height and good posture, Thomas certainly looked the part. To cement the ointment's new branding, the word 'family' was introduced to the headline. This was as cynical a move then as it is today. Families are a respectable demographic, often with a little money, and by pitching to them, Thomas was implying his product's safety and reliability, thereby engaging the housewife who controlled the family medicine chest. Plus, by affixing the word 'family' to his product, Thomas was carefully sidestepping Albinolo's error of naming syphilis as one of his favourite curable diseases. Self-conscious customers were likely to be put off by the prospect of asking for a blatant syphilis cure over the counter. Holloway's Universal Family Ointment was a respectable brand for a respectable clientele.

One of his first advertisements reads as follows:

Holloway's Universal Family Ointment will be found far more efficacious in the following diseases than any other remedy extant:– ulcers, venereal ulcers, wounds, bad legs, nervous pains, gout, rheumatism, contracted and stiff joints, pains in the chest and bones, difficult respiration, swellings and tumours, &c. Its effects have been astonishing in most severe cases of Stony and Ulcerated Cancers, Scrofula or King's Evil, in all skin diseases, as Ring Worm, Scald Head, &c, and in Burns, Soft Corns, Bunions, &c. 540 medical certificates, most of which are from the first medical authorities, such as Her Majesty's Sergeant Surgeon, Sir B.C. Brodie, Bart., and such like eminent names, must forever set at rest all doubt as to the superior efficacy of this remedy.

An endorsement from the Sergeant Surgeon would indeed be a coup. The letter accompanying this gushing ad comes however from a Herbert Mayo of Middlesex Hospital, claiming the ointment had worked in all cases he had used it, and he would soon be needing more. Mayo, a real professor of physiology and pathological anatomy, seems an unlikely candidate to be endorsing an unknown useless product, but around the time of Thomas contacting him, Mayo had just resigned from his position at King's College, having attempted and failed to jump ship to a rival institution. It is likely Thomas paid him for his letter. Soon, other testimonials from medical men appear to laud the Holloway name, including some cleverly recycled rejections of Albinolo's ointment. So politely had it been rejected, the letters were easily edited to look like endorsements.

Albinolo was livid. He took to the press, vigorously denying any affiliation with this Professor Holloway character popping up in all the daily papers.

CAUTION TO THE PUBLIC
MR FELIX ALBINOLO (from Turin), 23, Earl Street, Blackfriars, London, sole proprietor and compounder of the ointment called

> ALBINOLO'S OINTMENT warns the public that the testimonials of Sir Benjamin C. Brody, Bart, Herbert Mayo, Esq, Dr Wagner, J. Malyn, Esq, and Mister W.C. Dendy, Esq, (from which Mr Thomas Holloway of 13, Broad Street Buildings, City, gives garbled extracts in favour of a medicine of his own), referred to Albinolo's Ointment, and not to any discovery of Thomas Holloway, who never knew, nor was made acquainted with the ingredients of which Albinolo's Ointment is composed, or the secret to manufacturing the same.

Albinolo wrote to Herbert Mayo in the summer, apparently demanding to be given a similar testimonial. It looks as if he wasn't willing to pay, but the response was deemed lukewarm enough to pass as an endorsement:

> Sir–, I am much obliged to you for your polite offer to send me more of the ointment which I tried at Mr Holloway's request. I really have kept no note of its effects beyond what my communication to Mr Holloway contained. In a few cases of skin disease it was serviceable. The best case I had of its efficacy was one of scrofulous tubercules on the face of a child mended rapidly with it.

Damning with faint praise, Albinolo still published Mayo's letter in full. His desperation was showing. Soon, Holloway and Albinolo were at war in the press.

From Devon to John o'Groats, Albinolo poured his ire into the press.

> Felix Albinolo hereby cautions all persons against purchasing any ointment, or cerate (except his Ointment, called Albinolo's) as parties are publishing extracts of letters, which are below, in favour of another ointment, thereby misleading the public.

Albinolo was naïve. He freely published most of his ointment's recipe, even while claiming Thomas Holloway never knew its magical ingredients. Thomas must have laughed to read this claim, thinking of his mother's ruined coppers. The only winning blow either of them could make was to admit the ointment was nothing but pungent grease, and neither of them were prepared to go down with that ship.

Thomas coolly declined to comment on his one-time partner's accusations, but continued to publish furiously as Albinolo stepped up his own campaign. In some papers, the rivals appear alongside each other. Thomas went to the added expense of decorating his ads with illustrations, depicting a wise old man caring for the sick. Compared to Albinolo's hysterical allegations and mystical snakes, Thomas came out looking trustworthy.

10. A Holloway's trade card. The reverse features a collectable painting of an elephant. (Verity Holloway)

For all his rage on the subject of misleading the public, Albinolo dug up one of the letters of refusal from St Thomas's Hospital, using his rival's trick of editing it to look like an endorsement. The hospital threatened legal action. Perhaps they hadn't noticed Holloway's Ointment doing the same; nevertheless, they left him alone. With that final infuriating blow, Albinolo's passions overrode his common sense. His cautions to the public had failed to drum up the support he needed to subsist, and the printers' bills were far beyond his means. In one last push, he threw everything he had into his war with the Professor, as if he truly believed he could salvage his business, and his name. The public shrugged their shoulders. To them, Albinolo was just one more small-time quack yelling for attention.

If it gave Thomas Holloway any pleasure to know his former partner was penniless, that pleasure was short-lived. He, too, was broke.

Chapter 5

From Pills to Penury

Every failure teaches a man something, if he will learn.
Little Dorrit, Charles Dickens

By May 1840, Felix Albinolo was ruined. His name appears in *The Jurist*, alongside those of other insolvent debtors, who then were not seen as unfortunate victims of circumstance or bad decisions, but 'prisoners, whose Estates and Effects have been vested in the Provisional Assignee by Order of Court, having filed their Schedules, are ordered to be brought up before the Court, to be dealt with according to statute.' Albinolo's court date was 1 June. He shared it with a butcher, an innkeeper and an attorney's clerk who had fallen on hard times. His own title – 'ointment maker' – made him a novelty amongst his fellow debtors, but conveys little of his flamboyant past. The Italian was sentenced to debtors' gaol.

Thomas, too, had overreached himself. The newspaper proprietors publishing his advertisements had trusted him on the basis of his reputation for paying straight up for column space. One small favour led to another – irresistible little victories in the war against Albinolo – and before Thomas knew it, he had nothing. Like Albinolo, Thomas Holloway faced the court alongside his fellow humiliated debtors. Unlike many of them, he knew his predicament was entirely his own fault. For several weeks, the Professor had the extreme displeasure of being an inmate of Islington's Whitecross Street Prison for debtors.

Whitecross Street Prison was built in 1813 to house the overflow from London's infamous Newgate Prison. It housed 400 debtors until its closure in 1870, when remaining prisoners were transferred, somewhat ironically for Thomas, to Holloway Prison.

Debt was a crime for which the punishment made the situation worse. Prisons at this time were run for profit. The prisoner was expected to pay for his bed and food, his writing paper, and even heat. When the head of a family was sent to debtors' prison, his dependents suffered equally, as a 12-year-old Charles Dickens was unlucky enough to discover. His father was imprisoned in Marshalsea Debtors' Prison for owing money to a baker. Charles was removed from school and placed in a factory to earn money to support his father, and the experience had a lasting psychological effect. John Dickens was known as a kindly man, warm and hardworking, but part of the punishment for those who owed money was 'moral reeducation' consisting largely of forcing the prisoner to admit his inadequacies, real or otherwise. It left both the prisoner and his family utterly humiliated. Later, recalling how he had been sent to beg another inmate for the loan of a knife and fork to eat his dinner with, Charles wrote how his father urged him to take care with money: 'If a man had twenty pounds a year and spent nineteen pounds, nineteen shillings and sixpence, he would be happy; but a shilling spent more would make him wretched.'

It was an easy fate to fall into. The social stigma of a family man having failed to manage his finances was huge, and Charles Dickens lived with the lasting shadow for the rest of his life, as if debt were a ghost that could intrude at any moment.

> My whole nature was so penetrated with grief and humiliation … that even now, famous and caressed and happy, I often forget in my dreams that I have a dear wife and children; even that I am a man; and wander desolately back to that time of my life.

With its stony exterior, square and austere as any castle, Whitecross Street Prison was a shock to Thomas Holloway's system. In some contemporary illustrations, the building is shown to have grates either side of the front door at the level of the pavement for the poorest inmates to reach out their hands to passersby, begging for pennies to pay their way. Newgate, the 'gloomy depository of the guilt and misery of London', had ceased to be a debtors' gaol for some years before Thomas's insolvency. However, it was common knowledge that the door condemned men walked through on their way to the gallows was still called Debtors' Door. Debt was a kind of death, and prison was the purgatory offering rebirth.

This shadow of ruin hanging over the unfortunate debtor made the debtors' prison an obvious setting for the cheap, nasty 'penny bloods', the pulp fiction of the age. One popular series, *Mysteries of London*, which covered the infamous Bethlem asylum and the grisly adventures of the body snatchers, had an issue devoted to Whitecross in which a decent young fellow, Chichester, finds himself behind bars. In typical penny blood style, there is a great deal of weeping and rain and gin-drenched tales of injustice, but the details about the everyday workings of the prison are sound. On a dark and stormy night, Chichester is led through the gates Thomas himself had to pass through to his punishment:

> Chichester was then introduced into a large room containing ten or a dozen beds, whose frame-work was made of iron. One miserably thin blanket, a horse-cloth, and a straw mattress and pillow, were all provided for each couch, by the Corporation of the City of London!
>
> Oh! how generous – how philanthropic – how noble to tear men away from their homes and give them straw, wrapped up in coarse ticking, to sleep upon!

The pity of the benevolent rich was all part of the punishment. At the behest of Charles II's mistress, Nell Gwynne, one lucky Whitecross debtor would be released every Christmas Day, his debts covered by £20. For those not fortunate enough to be bailed out by a long-dead royal mistress, a large board bearing the names of local philanthropists was displayed for all prisoners to see, reminding them who was paying for their bed and board, and also giving them something to live up to. 'Your mistakes put you here,' it prompted them, and as long as he lived, Thomas never forgot it.

Mysteries of London wasn't all sensation. Like most melodrama, written or performed, it carried a strong message of the injustice faced by the lower classes, who were powerless to protest:

> The system of imprisonment for debt is in itself impolitic, unwise, and cruel in the extreme:– it ruins the honest man, and destroys the little remnant of good feeling existing in the heart of the callous one. It establishes the absurd doctrine, that if a man cannot pay his debts while he is allowed the exercise of his talents, his labour, and his acquirements, he can when shut up in the narrow compass of a prison, where his talents, his labour, and his acquirements are useless. How eminently narrow-sighted are English legislators! They fear totally to abolish this absurd custom, because they dread that credit will suffer. Why – credit is altogether begotten in confidence, and never arises from the preconceived intention on the part of him who gives it, to avail himself of this law against him who receives it. Larceny and theft are punished by a limited imprisonment, with an allowance of food; but debtors, who commit no crime, may linger and languish – and starve in gaol.

The popular view of debtors leaned towards the image of the libertine and the gambler, rather than the unlucky ordinary man or woman. At Whitecross, Thomas would have found himself amongst all kinds of men, with a vast array of stories behind them:

> The Poultry Ward was a long, dark, low room, with seven or eight barred windows on each side, sawdust upon the stone floor, and about a dozen or fourteen small tables arranged, like those of a coffee house, around the walls. The room was full of debtors of all appearances – from the shabby-genteel down to the absolutely ragged. Here a prisoner was occupied in drawing up his schedule for the Insolvent Debtors' Court;– there an emaciated old man was writing a letter, over which he shed bitter and scalding tears;– at another table a young farmer's labourer-looking man was breakfasting off bread

and cheese and onions, which he washed down with porter;– close
by was a stout, seedy looking person with grey hair, who did not
seem to have any breakfast at all;– in this nook a poor pale wretch
was reading a newspaper;– in that corner another individual was
examining a pile of letters;– several were gathered round the fire.

Thomas may have shed scalding tears over his folly, but he didn't
have time to starve. It wasn't long before his mother came to his
aid. She paid his bail and half his debts, once his creditors were
assured of her eldest son's previous good character.

Albinolo was not so fortunate. On his release, he attempted to
re-establish himself as a successful figure in the patent medicine
business, dropping the Catholic allusions and mystical imagery.
But for all his years of advertising and hustling, Albinolo gradually
slides out of sight. He was evidently still bitter in 1865. Half of his
ad space in *The Working Man* was dedicated to his old partner:

> Thomas Holloway, formerly interpreter to ALBINOLO, has sold in
> the United Kingdom and the different countries of the Globe some
> millions worth of the spurious imitation of this wonderful Ointment.

It was no use. By then, Thomas was securely a household name,
and few would believe a ranting foreigner had ever been in
business with him. Rumour claimed Albinolo died insane, which
gives his story a rather Dickensian gloss of moral judgement. In
fact, he remained in London with his son, trying for many years
to establish himself as a rival to Holloway. It was never to be; in
the 1870s, we last see Albinolo wandering Soho. Known as a local
character, he wore his Napoleonic medal with pride, showing it to
anyone who would listen, insisting how alike he and the Emperor
were in looks. Reading between the lines, it would appear Albinolo
became something of a beggar, or heavily reliant, at least, on the
charity of the Soho residents who knew his story. It seems he died
around this time, poor and understandably bitter. An obituary of
sorts in the *Echo* suggests he never stopped telling people how he

was double-crossed by his 'interpreter': 'The interpreter seems to have proved himself more clever than the inventor; for, while the former is now at the head of a large firm, the latter is probably on his death-bed in an hospital.'

On his way home with Mrs Holloway, in need of a bath and some decent food, we can only wonder which Thomas felt more keenly: relief or shame. Whatever awkward conversation followed on the way home from Whitecross, Thomas made a vow he would keep for the rest of his days: no debts left unpaid. Even in his eighties, he was known as a supremely trustworthy man where money was concerned. Which is just as well, because soon Thomas would literally have more money than he knew what to do with.

Chapter 6

'Ha! Ha! Cured in an instant!'

There's nothing like a stretch behind bars to give a man a little perspective. Thomas knew he had to shape up, in all areas of life. First, he purchased a shop on the Strand; number 244, which can be seen in the far left of the picture, overleaf, emblazoned with the Holloway name. The whole family moved in, and all were expected to chip in to Thomas's fledgling business.

Thomas's younger brother Henry was evidently at a loose end. He was enlisted to visit chemist and druggist's, asking for Holloway's Ointment. When the shop assistants said they had never heard of such a product, Henry made a scene. Did they *want* their customers to suffer? The following day, Thomas would go to the shop posing as a wholesaler, smoothly securing a deal. Sometimes, if Henry was unavailable, Thomas would attempt both roles himself, providing a different member of staff was on duty.

The manufacturing legwork was down to Thomas, too:

My beginning was in a small way – my task very difficult and disheartening. I may add, as proof of my early discouragement, that I had expended in one week the sum of £100 in advertising, and various other ways, for the purposes of my business, and all I sold in that time was two small pots of Ointment. In fact, no person would then have accepted the Medicines as a gift. I had to practise the most rigid economy and to work most assiduously. By four o'clock each morning I had generally commenced my day not to cease until ten at night, in order to do that myself for which I must else have paid others.

11. The Strand during Thomas Holloway's residency. On the far left, his shop and its signs are visible. From *Original Views of London as it is*, by Thomas Shotter Boys, 1842.
(Verity Holloway)

Before the Albinolo debacle, Thomas had taken the initiative to add pills to his repertoire, getting a clerk at 13 Broad Street to help him with a small pill-making device in the cellar. The pills were a typical simple nostrum: little more than a mild laxative with added spices. On taking the prescribed handful, a consumer might experience some rumblings down below and take it to mean the medicine was working. Pill-making was fiddly work, and easy to do badly. An apothecary would take a basic recipe and multiply it depending on the number of pills he required, first grinding the ingredients with a mortar and pestle and then mixing them with glucose or other sticky agents to form a dough. It is doubtful Thomas was quite so exact to begin with, especially as money was tight, but as his pills contained no antimony or opium, a little sloppiness was perfectly acceptable. After the grinding, he would take a 'pill tile' and roll the mixture into a sausage, which could then be sliced into equal segments, like old-fashioned peppermints. These were then rolled into balls and left to dry. A sugary coating could then be added, but as that meant further expense, Thomas probably let his customers taste a little bitterness. To add levity to this tedious work, Thomas and his clerk would sing together and later celebrate with supper. This arrangement, he later claimed, happily went on for years.

Happiness, it seemed, was here to stay. In 1840, Thomas married the pretty, sober Miss Jane Pearce Driver, the 26-year-old daughter of a Rotherhithe shipwright. It is probable the pair met while Thomas was attempting to hawk ointment to sailors. The nautical theme ran through their courtship. Thomas gave Jane the pet name 'Grace Darling' after the heroic young woman who helped her lighthouse keeper father save nine shipwrecked people in 1838. An instant celebrity, Grace Darling was flooded with gifts and marriage proposals, and so too did Jane find herself the object of a dynamic young man's affections. A billet-doux from their courting years offers an endearing glimpse into Thomas's softer side:

If Grace Darling can have the permission of her Parents to go to
Drury Lane this Evening she must be here by half past five o'clock.

Grace will find that plenty of Tea and Toast well stowed away
in her Lighthouse before she leaves King Street will enable her
Lamp to be in good trim all evening.

Holloway's umbrella will be as useful to him tonight as a Pot of
Ointment to a bad leg.

Here is proof of Thomas's commercial realism. He knew – and
didn't mind Jane knowing – that his medicine was useless. This
clear-headed attitude may well have been what Albinolo fatally
lacked. Influencing people's minds was the most important part
of the patent medicine trade. Ethics aside, Victorian physicians
were aware of the placebo effect. If we are to be kind to Thomas,
we might imagine he believed in the psychological efficacy of his
products. The alternative is to paint him as a villain. Neither seems
to fit the man he was at this point in his life. He certainly never
mocked his customers in any surviving paperwork, and the instant
support he gained from Jane and the entire Driver family suggests
his enthusiasm for the fledgling business was infectious.

In the following few years, Thomas kept up his punishing work
schedule. Jane, it seemed, not only didn't mind a few privations,
but threw herself into the production line at the Strand, lending
a hand to grind ingredients and roll them into pills. Like her
husband, she saw the potential of the business, and the need for
as much money as possible to be ploughed into advertising. When
Thomas's mother died on 26 March 1843, she left Thomas a house
on the Strand and one in Penzance, giving him an income from
rent, plus releasing him of any debts to her, including the one that
bailed him out of Whitecross. This inheritance allowed Thomas
to recommence his assault on the press and the brickwork of
London.

Helpfully, a miracle occurred: 'An astonishing cure of the Earl
of Aldborough, by this miraculous medicine! After every other

means had failed!!' So went one of Thomas's most widely circulated advertisements. Not an instantly recognizable name, this Earl of Aldborough, but nevertheless an endorsement Thomas was willing to plaster anywhere and everywhere possible:

> SIR – Various circumstances prevented the possibility of my thanking you before this time for your politeness in sending me your pills as you did. I now take this opportunity of sending you an order for the amount, and, at the same time to add that your pills have effected a cure of a disorder in my Liver and Stomach, which all the most eminent of the Faculty at home, and all over the continent, had not been able to effect; nay, not even the waters of Carlsbad and Marienbad. I wish to have another box and a pot of ointment, in case any of my family should ever require either.
>
> Your most obliged and obedient Servant.

So ubiquitous was the Earl's gratitude, particularly on walls already choked with bill stickers, *Punch* noticed. In one of their acidic takes on the public 'artworks' of small-time quacks, Professor Holloway's miracles receive a special mention:

> Among the earliest exhibitions of the present season, that of the Bill Stickers stands exceedingly high, and is replete with a truly charming variety. The pictorial placard has opened out quite a new style of art, and we shall not be surprised to find some of the first painters of the age devoting their genius to the composition of broadsides. One of the earliest efforts in this direction was the celebrated 'Ha! Ha! Cured in an instant!' which will be found in the collection of Professor HOLLOWAY, who was certainly a greater professor – looking at his professions – than the rest of his contemporaries. It will be remembered that his ointment was warranted to pull out teeth, extract corns, demolish bunions, remove baldness, get rid of gout, produce whiskers, cure indigestion, give an appetite, take away freckles, soften the hands, prolong life, arch the eyebrows, support the knees, eradicate chaps from the lips, and promote activity in the muscles.

The Earl of Aldborough is no doubt the nobleman whose portrait is exhibited in the celebrated 'Ha! Ha!' tableau, for the aristocratic patient is continually sending up to the Professor the details of some astonishing cure which has been produced by the marvelous ointment.

The Earl of Aldborough must have been a wonderful man to have gone through so many dangers, and the wonderful ointment is worthy of the noble who appears to live upon it. We cannot deny to the Professor the credit of having been one of the first to associate the fine arts with advertising hand-bills, and thus to lay the foundation for those exhibitions of puffing pictures which give new life to all the dead walls in and about the metropolis.

The Earl in question was Mason Gerard Stratford, 5th Earl of Aldborough. *Punch* magazine was still using the Earl for comic fuel well into the 1880s. Known for his love of patent medicines, he came from a long line of Irish eccentrics, soon doomed to die out. A bigamist with several children and a consumptive wife to support, Mason was frequently desperate for money. His stock trick was to visit moneylenders with a loaded gun and threaten to shoot himself if they did not grant him a loan. His apparent zeal for Holloway's pills may have had something to do with the fact that Thomas was paying the rent on his sunny Leghorn accommodation. The Earl died in 1849, by which time his endorsements were considered hilarious. In a cartoon by George Cruikshank entitled *The Sick Goose and the Council of Health*, a dying goose – 'goose' being slang for idiot – is visited by a troupe of quacks, one of whom, an anthropomorphic jar of ointment, says, 'His case is exactly like the Earl of Aldborough's so nothing can cure him but Holloway's Ointment & Pills.' Another *Punch* cartoon showed the Earl as a tiny figure futilely trying to escape from a jar of pills.

THERE ARE NONE OF US SAFE!
There seems to be no escape from PROFESSOR HOLLOWAY. For some time, he had got a live earl shut up in the Villa Messina

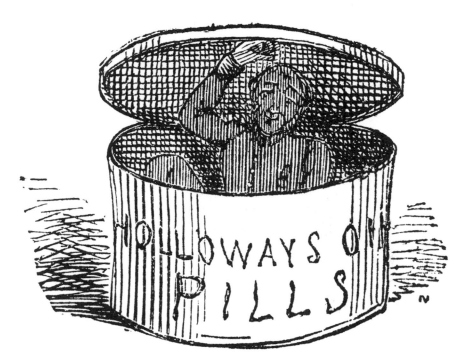

12. An 1849 *Punch* joke at the Earl of Adlborough's expense. A hapless debtor and bigamist, there wasn't much the Earl wasn't prepared to do for money.
(Verity Holloway)

at Florence, swallowing pills by the hundred, and writing letters by the score, to say what benefit he derived in all the maladies under the sun – and the sun is very comprehensive at Florence. This week PROFESSOR HOLLOWAY has got into his hands a Waterloo hero's legs, which had been changed into all colours by rheumatic gout; so that, if not bow legs, they were positively rainbow legs in one respect, at all events. HOLLOWAY evidently sets his ointment – as bird-catchers set bird-lime – for all the 'bad legs' in the world to hop on to it. We understand that the Professor is setting a trap for the Pope's leg-ate, in the event of Ambassadors being exchanged, and will undertake the cure of soles to any extent, under the pontifical patronage.

Since his spat with Albinolo, Thomas seemed to have grown out of bristling at the first sign of a challenge. The satire merely proved

13. *Thomas Holloway*, 1845, oil on canvas, William Wallace Scott. (© Royal Holloway, University of London)

14. Jane Holloway, 1845, oil on canvas, William Wallace Scott. (© Royal Holloway, University of London)

his name was becoming well known, and by that time, money was steadily coming in. In 1845, he and Jane were sufficiently rich to have their portraits painted by William Scott. Thomas stands before a pastoral background, smiling slightly, his black curly hair fashionably coiffeured. He looks content yet ambitious, with his jeweled tie pin hinting at the comforts of newfound wealth. In her portrait, Jane looks straight on, supplementing her sober black outfit with lace and several ornate items of jewellery. Her tiny left hand points towards her wedding ring, indicating the source of her prosperity.

Both husband and wife look serene and respectable, only slightly at odds with Thomas's decision to advertise in the *Town*, a publication known for its salacious articles on prostitutes, dirty poems and the advertising of illegal prize fights. So too had Thomas utilised the art of product placement in low theatres and gaffs, where men went to pick up good-time girls and generally let loose of an evening. Although the middle-class family was a rich market for patent medicines, the lower classes were not to be ignored, as Poor Man's Friend ointment had already proved. The veneer of moral disgust spread thinly over the *Town's* dubious pages offered plausible deniability for readers and advertisers alike. Plus, the venerable Earl of Aldborough would hardly endorse a product aimed at lowlife. Thomas was merely being pragmatic in spreading his net widely, a strategy that paid dividends.

Early on, he adopted novel forms of advertising, including song sheets of popular ballads emblazoned with his wares. Copper coins were minted to act as gift vouchers, and most were sent to Australia to act as early colonial currency. Tails depicted the usual image of Hygeia on her throne, while Thomas himself acted as the head, turned in stern profile with his hair full and curly. He is labelled as Professor Thomas Holloway, but the illiterate would be forgiven for mistaking the man for a king. The fact that Thomas was using his own face signalled a new age for Holloway's Ointment and Pills. Thomas, or at least his professor alter ego, was becoming the face of his own brand.

15. An 1858 Holloway's token coin.
(Verity Holloway)

As profits increased, so did Thomas's ambitions. By 1848, Holloway's Ointment and Pills were appearing in publications across the planet. In New Zealand, they were heralded as 'THE GREATEST CURES OF ANY MEDICINE IN THE GLOBE'. Testimonials from local sources raved. For curing his wife of rheumatism, a Mister James Rochford of Little Bally Bong wished his testimonial to be published 'for the sake of humanity'. Interpreters were brought in to translate copy into Arabic, Sanskrit, Chinese, Turkish, and various Indian dialects. Thomas was heralded as 'the mighty healer' and the 'healing genius' – mainly by himself, of course, but that didn't matter to his customers, who were placing orders in their thousands. It was said that intrepid Englishmen visiting the newly fashionable pyramids of Giza were greeted by a gigantic advert for Holloway's Pills, as if the pharaohs themselves were giving their testimonial. Another apocryphal story has a young soldier remarking that the strangest thing about his arrival in Fiji was the sign at the port informing him Holloway's Pills were now available on the island. As Dickens had prophesied, the name of Thomas Holloway was inescapable.

Such a feat doesn't happen by sitting behind a desk. Knowing the effect of his height and quiet charm, Thomas was intent on setting foot in the newspaper offices of as many nations as he could afford. In 1848, Jane accompanied Thomas on a grand tour of sorts, stretching from Dover to Moscow. Visiting a new city almost every day was typical of Thomas's energy levels. At times, reading his travel diary, one pities his wife. Thomas scheduled practically no down time, travelling overnight by train or stagecoach to meet appointments the following morning, often sleeping and eating on the go. When they weren't travelling or negotiating advertising space, Thomas was determined to give Jane speedy glimpses of the major landmarks and points of interest each town had to offer. 4 June in Leyden, Holland, was a typical day:

Visited the Town Hall where is the historical Picture of Van der Werff of the Seige of 1574. Saw the Catholic and Protestant Churches ... the University, The Museum of Natural History and that of Antiquities. Also a private museum of a Medical gentleman who was many years in Japan. There is a famous Botanical Garden in this Town which I saw. The Fair was here.

Unsurprisingly, after a month of this, his exhausted wife negotiated some solo time back in London. Thomas was melancholy in her absence, and reflected, 'God bless her she is one of the best of Wifes[1] any man ever had.' He cheered himself up at six the next morning with a 12-mile walk across the hills of Bad Ems, in Rheinland, Germany.

Despite longing for Jane and hating having to stay in so many 'Dirty and Dististible [sic]' hotels, the trip was a huge success. With pure self-puffery, Thomas managed to secure orders for a staggering amount of medicine, across Europe and beyond. Handbills were distributed in dozens of languages, and those all-important advertising contracts were secured, even in Russia, whom Britain had been fighting only a few years before. The reach of advertising had been growing wider and more powerful throughout the eighteenth and nineteenth centuries, but Thomas Holloway was one of the first businessmen to make it his entire focus. This was a huge gamble for a product that was essentially worthless, but also a very modern one, working on the principal that if the public are hammered with a message long enough, and steadily enough, they will eventually be wooed – consciously, or unconsciously.

Reunited with Jane at home in London, Thomas already had his sights set on South America. With some charm and some hard work, his name was now a global brand. The days of hawking free samples to sailors were long gone.

---

1   Reading Thomas's private papers, I have come across a few Cornish phonetic spellings, hinting Thomas never lost his native accent. He writes charmingly of 'Cathederals' with 'belferries'.

Chapter 7

Prosperity and Other Curses

Prosperity moves families in strange ways. Henry Holloway had hitherto been a willing participant in his elder brother's business, but after Thomas's marriage to Jane, relations began to shift. Thomas became increasingly involved with the Driver family and less so with his own. Long after his death, Thomas's employees considered it common knowledge he vastly preferred the company of his wife's relations to the Holloways, though the whys and wherefores remain mysterious.

Henry Holloway evidently found living under his prosperous brother's shadow too much to bear. It appears he left London for Hampshire – his birth county – some time before the Albinolo debacle boiled over. County court records show a Henry Holloway of the correct age as being acquitted of larceny in Southampton in 1838. Whether or not this was Thomas's brother is hard to tell for certain, but Henry was subsequently excluded from his mother's will. Working as gardener to a Reverend Vaux in Southampton, this same Henry Holloway raised prize-winning fruit and vegetables, but was evidently prone to a hot temper. In 1834 he was sent to gaol for two months for assaulting a man, and was later fined for drunkenly fighting with an acquaintance after breaking into his house. Shortly after his acquittal for larceny in 1838 in the same county, a William Henry Holloway filed for insolvency. Serial offenders would commonly use middle names or rearrange their initials to avoid leaving a paper trail.

We could surmise the shame of her son being accused of such a disgraceful crime as petty theft prompted Mrs Holloway to cut

Henry off. After all, even being acquitted would cast a shadow on the family name. Considering her hasty rescue of Thomas from Whitecross Prison, the disinheritance must have been doubly hurtful for Henry. By the time Thomas's star was on the rise, Henry was married and in dire need of funds.

And so London found itself home to two Holloway's Pills & Ointment companies.

Like his brother, Henry knew an opportunity when he saw one. He set up shop just a few doors down the street from Thomas. Same name, same product, same locale. Thomas was shocked by the brazenness of it all. Henry could easily have gone into business with Thomas; they had made a good team before. Why go to the trouble of this foolishness? Henry refused to back down when his brother confronted him. With the same stubbornness of Holloway vs Albinolo, Henry protested that his jars bore the initial H, making them easily distinguishable from any other company of similar name. It was pure cheek, and when Henry refused to respond to

16. Holloway's Ointment jars. The cherub sometimes held a sign reading 'Don't despair!' (Science Museum, London. Wellcome Images)

reason or brotherly cajoling, Thomas did precisely what Henry was banking on him not doing: he summoned the lawyers.

The court transcript shows that Henry had gone to considerable lengths to be mistaken for his brother:

> This was a motion by the plaintiff, Thomas Holloway, for an injunction to restrain the defendant, Henry Holloway, his servants and agents, from selling or exposing for sale, or causing or procuring to be sold, any pills or ointment described or purporting to be 'Holloway's pills or Holloway's ointment or H. Holloway's pills or H. Holloway's ointment', in boxes or pots, having affixed thereto, or burnt or stamped thereon, such labels as were in the plaintiff's bill of complaint mentioned, or any other labels so contrived or expressed as by colourable imitation to represent the pills or ointment, and also from printing or publishing the pamphlets or direction papers and from using the wrappers in the plaintiff's said bill also mentioned, or any other pamphlets, directions, papers, or wrappers, so composed, expressed, prepared, or contrived so as to represent that any pills or ointment sold by the defendant were the same as the pills and ointment sold by the plaintiff.

While Henry was able to prove that his recipes had been bought from a medical student, the accompanying papers and instructions were undeniably almost identical to Thomas's. Pill cutters and vendors approached by Henry came forward in court to say they had refused his business for fear of accusations of fraud. So too had the Commissioners of Stamps – the body in charge of licensing patent medicines – refused to grant Henry the same stamp as his brother. Worse, Thomas claimed Henry had admitted to his face the intention of fraud. Thomas wasn't the only one. Multiple parties testified that Henry knowingly engineered the fraud. He had also spent plenty of money. Half of a Strand shop window had already been hired out to display Henry's wares, despite the owner pointing out the danger in mimicking Thomas's brand. Henry replied that the public would never notice the difference.

Whether it was stubbornness or desperation, Henry was well aware of the situation and had pressed on regardless, practically goading his brother to take him to court.

Henry at least did his best to appear respectable before the judge, Lord Langdale. Rather than go into business with Thomas, he grandly spoke of having set up his own manufactory. Perhaps the possibility of being his brother's employee was too much for Henry's pride, a feeling most second sons could relate to. Nevertheless, as the press gleefully reported, the factory turned out to be two shabby rented rooms, both of which were empty. After rent, Henry could only afford £1 a week on advertising, whereas Thomas had spent £150,000 on global advertising and planned to continue. Despite Henry's protestations, anyone with any common sense could see he was hoping to benefit from that gigantic advertising budget. Henry had gone so far as to take up his old role as stooge, entering chemist and druggist's shops pretending to offer the bona fide Holloway's Pills at a discount. Henry was a parasite on a much larger beast.

More concerning was the testimony of one Amy Newberry, who claimed to have relied on Thomas Holloway's pills for a year as an effective cure for dropsy. On two occasions, she purchased Henry's pills in error, and both times fell ill. On examination, the pills contained no potentially harmful ingredients, but were so significantly different to Thomas's recipe that a habitual user may have found them injurious. This must have been especially galling to Henry, who knew as well as his brother how effective their medicines truly were.

Interestingly, in the press coverage of the trial there is no mention of the medical merits of either man's product. In fact, Thomas received praise for his pills, which, for some years, were said to have had 'high repute with the public for their curative and healing qualities … in all quarters of the globe'. Perhaps Thomas thought it prudent to persuade a few reporters to put in a good word – these papers did, after all, print his testimonials. This Holloway vs

Holloway affair was an unavoidably personal embarrassment, but Thomas somehow prevented it from becoming a black mark on his professional life. As injured as he may have felt, Thomas was – in all things – shrewd.

Lord Langdale said he had never seen a clearer case of its kind, and although Henry protested he had not been given time to properly answer the charges, the injunction was granted. It was effectively the end of the brothers' relationship. Henry all but vanishes from Thomas's papers for decades, bar a few sparse mentions of 'poor Henry'. He died poor in 1874 in Marylebone, having repeatedly refused Thomas's offers of financial aid.

Thomas Holloway had become the kind of man who would sue his own brother. But what did that really mean? It has since been said that Thomas was an uncommunicative man at the best of times, given to coolness, and preferring business to leisure. This may well be because he and Jane had no children, generating the oft-quoted letter to his sister Caroline, who lived in one of Thomas's properties: 'Whoever may go down to see you, must bring no children with them. I will never have any in my house as you know and you shall have none in yours. Upon this point I am most positive.' Taken on face value, this remark by the ageing businessman sounds like the edict of a bitter man, but there is no evidence to suggest he and Jane had not tried for a baby and failed. Building an empire as successfully as Thomas had inevitably generated gossip as to who would inherit. Thomas had a melancholy temperament, and a need to be in control. The sights and sounds of children in his house – even in a house he did not live in – may well have been a source of anxiety, or even pain.

Later, referring to the completion of Holloway College, the architect William Henry Crossland remarked: 'He seldom, or perhaps never, praised anyone.' A pat on the back and an understated 'I am more than pleased' was the height of compliments. But Crossland was an associate, not one of Thomas's near and dear. The falling-out with Henry didn't preclude him from maintaining good relationships.

Most of the Drivers became involved in the business over the following years in a way the Holloways never would. When Thomas became a rich man with property to match, he and Jane opened their doors to Jane's sisters, the unmarried Mary Ann (who, to Thomas, was always 'Polly') and Sarah, ('Sally') with her husband George Martin, who quickly struck up a rapport with Thomas that would last to the end of his days. Along with George and Sarah's daughter Celia, they created the kind of mutually supportive extended family unit that was common for the nineteenth century. Indeed, by the time Thomas reached his seventies and could no longer keep up with correspondence, he makes reference to his private secretary, who was, in fact, Celia Martin. Looking back from the 1940s, Celia's husband recalled how she was treated by Thomas and Jane as an adopted daughter as well as an active and valued member of 'the dear old firm'. Celia must have been a quick study – Thomas was notorious for gathering three or four clerks (on especially manic days, up to half a dozen) and dictating several letters at once.

As the company grew, his staff were always treated like family, with their well-being as a top priority. There is no better proof of Thomas's warmth than his concern for those on his payroll. Sometimes, however, Thomas was forced to employ some tough love. The general habit of firms paying workers cash in hand in large weekly or monthly sums meant that many men fell to the temptations of the pub. Public houses offered heat, light, entertainment and company, and peer pressure from colleagues made it easy for a man to blow most of his wage before it reached his wife. The Temperance Movement, active from the 1830s until the early twentieth century, targeted working-class men in particular. Texts like J. Ewing Ritchie's 1857 *The Night Side of London* demonised the leisure habits of the poor for the entertainment of their wealthier – and therefore morally righteous – neighbours. A drink in a respectable public house was perfectly acceptable, Ritchie wrote, provided one remained courteous and in control of one's faculties. Drinking establishments for the working man, however, were described in terms of horror:

> So hideous is the life, so degraded the company, so revolting are the scenes, at these night-houses, I know not why the law permits them to be open. I am sure they can answer no good or moral end.

As in all Victorian melodrama, to flirt with immorality is to court death, no matter how innocent the intention:

> You and I know that if the man had not gone into the respectable public-house he might have lived another ten years – that it was because he went there night after night, and sat soaking there night after night, that the blood-vessels became gorged and clotted, and that the wonderful machine stood still. 'Poisoned by alcohol' is the true verdict – by alcohol sold and consumed in the respectable public-house. How long will society sanction such places? How long will they retard the progress of the nation by wasting energies, and time, and cash, and opportunities that might have been devoted to nobler ends? How long with their splendour – with their gilding and glass – with their air of respectability and comfort, will they attract the unwary, ruin the weak, and slay the strong man in his strength and pride?

Whilst plenty of Temperance Movement members undeniably enjoyed the sense of superiority gained from telling the poor what they may and may not do, some had nobler ambitions. Instead of frightening people with tales of gin-soaked doom, they chose instead to appeal to working men's sense of pride; to challenge the prevailing concept of masculinity to include a demonstration of self-control, particularly when it came to drink. Addiction was not a recognised problem; dependence on alcohol was seen as a moral failing. Men were encouraged to 'take the pledge' – literally sign a contract dedicated to God – either swearing off excessive consumption or taking the more extreme decision to eschew alcohol entirely, even at home. The pledge had religious and political ramifications. Teetotalers and temperate men were encouraged to get involved in grassroots politics to improve the conditions of the working classes, with the hope of enabling some form of social mobility in the future – trading the loss of control that comes with alcohol for an attempt to steer their own destinies.

This was pie-in-the-sky nonsense to the average man collecting his wage, and Thomas Holloway knew it. Having grown up in a pub, he understood that a convivial drink was a normal and healthy part of the working-class life, and that denying his employees this ritual as some employers attempted to would not make him popular. However, rewards for self-control outside the workplace were an important part of working for Holloway. When an employee of his – a man with the most Dickensian surname of Rough – transpired to be spending more than half his wage on drink, Thomas was moved to personally admonish him. The paleness of Rough's neglected children, Thomas noted in a letter, was most upsetting to witness. Thereafter, it became the custom at Holloway's for employees to be paid daily, to reduce the temptation to go on a spree and to help wives economise at home. Thomas was a firm believer in helping people help themselves, not providing handouts. Charity, he said time and time again, demeaned the recipient, and personal pride what was a man needed to prosper.

Pensions, too, were a perk of working for Holloway's – so long as you were well behaved at work and at home. Each employee, male and female, who had worked for Thomas for eighteen years would receive an annuity of £20 on retirement, providing they never fell foul of the police or went bankrupt. It is easy to see shades of Thomas's Whitecross Prison fiasco in this decision. An annual £20 was just enough to live on, roughly the same annual sum as a servant would receive, and comparable to today's state pension. It was a safety net to keep debt at bay, not a windfall. There was virtually no social security in Victorian Britain, and private pensions, rare as they were, were a godsend for the aged and those without children to support them. For the sick, doctors' bills were a grim prospect, so Thomas made sure a doctor (a real one) was on hand to oversee the health of his staff, and any individual too sick to work would be financially taken care of during their infirmity. Long after Thomas's death, Marion Krause remembered how her grandfather was chosen for a post at Holloway's despite being noticeably poorer than the other applicants. When sciatica prevented him from working, the company made sure he had a pound a week up until his death in 1912. By the standards of Victorian employment, Holloway's was excellent, for workers and their dependents.

By the time of Henry Holloway's injunction, Thomas's business was expanding at an incredible rate. Money no longer being a problem, Thomas was free to extend his premises and his payroll. Extensions were added to the Strand shop, which attracted a great deal of local attention for its grand and imposing appearance,

 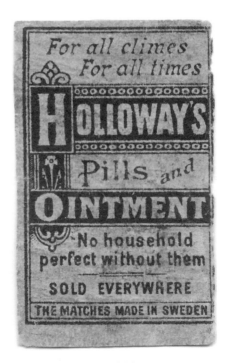

17. Matchboxes were another convenient marketing vehicle.
(Verity Holloway)

plastered with the Holloway name and testimonials to the Professor's healing genius. Cheekily, Thomas had persuaded the Museum of the Royal Pharmaceutical Society to hand out fliers to visitors bearing the testimonial of one ecstatic Irishman:

> Two years ago I lost the use of my limbs – they were quite benumbed; my sight was becoming numbed, my hearing dull, and pains which had plagued me for twenty years were growing worse. I consulted the more eminent of the faculty without deriving any benefit. About a month since I was induced to try your Pills and Ointment, and I feel myself in duty bound to make known to you and the public the miraculous change they wrought in me in a few days. On the fourth day I perceived a change for the better; my pulse began to beat stronger, the blood to circulate more freely than it had flown for years, my sight to receive its former clearness, and my hearing as acute as ever. I am now, thanks to God and your invaluable Pills and Ointment, quite recovered.

Holloway's Pills and Ointment, on a par with God. Presumably, the Museum of the Royal Pharmaceutical Society needed a cash injection. The following year, 1867, the Strand buildings were too small, necessitating a move to the newly created New Oxford Street, which had smashed a gentrified path straight through the infamous Gin Lane slums of St Giles. There, in a grand corner building with vaulted windows, Thomas set up what sounds more like an embassy than a patent medicine manufactory. Replete with a luxurious dining hall, baths and library, the new headquarters had its own printing press and a bevy of gentlemen (either by birth or education) fluent in every language imaginable, ready to assist any foreign visitor interested in their health. Naturally, it attracted flocks of the press, who were treated with the utmost civility. Professor Holloway, they said, was the kind of man more businessmen ought to emulate.

In 1878, Thomas published a 'Medical Guide for the use of missionaries and others who kindly interest themselves in recommending the use of his remedies', in which he wrote: 'The prevention and cure of disease is a matter of vital importance to all mankind.' In the manufactory and in the home, Professor Holloway was styling himself as a humanitarian. However, no successful man is without enemies, particularly a man who makes his fortune in the business of quackery.

Chapter 8

Quacks, Plague Take Them

Armed for virtue when I point the pen
Brand the bold front of shameless guilty men:
Hear this and tremble! You who 'scape the laws.

Alexander Pope

As long as they have existed, quacks have had their opponents. On numerous occasions throughout the nineteenth century, leading figures from the medical profession attempted to club together and discredit the likes of Thomas Holloway. In 1853, *The Medical Circular* asked the obvious question:

> The public prosecutor has commenced proceedings before the Tribunal of Police in Paris, against not fewer than eleven somnambulists on the charge of illegally practising Medicine … Why have we not a public prosecutor in England, and the power to prosecute quacks before a magistrate?

Such legislation – as sensible as it was – was simply not the British way. Although some punters listened when the medical establishment warned them to exercise some common sense, the outcome was always the same – as long as doctors were the reserve of the wealthy, an affordable pill or ointment was the working man's friend, despite its ingredients. Word of mouth was a powerful marketing tool for alternative medicine, and still is. A great boon for Victorian quacks was the widespread habit of taking several remedies at once, even alongside the advice of a physician. If the patient was lucky enough to get better, it was impossible to say which remedy was the victor. Holloway's Pills and Ointment somehow gathered a devoted following

PUNCH, OR THE LONDON CHARIVARI.—December 17, 1864.

A QUACK IN THE RIGHT PLACE;
Or, What we Should Like to See.

18. The quacks' uncanny ability to evade justice was an outrage to those who knew the
true dangers of patent medicine. *Punch*, 1864.
(Wellcome Library, London)

of customers, who, as we have already seen, were willing to testify
to their efficacy in court.

At the very least, physicians wanted to warn the public about the
presence of harmful chemicals in patent medicines and the dangers

of unqualified individuals mixing up nostrums. If inefficacy couldn't sway them, perhaps self-preservation would. Countless court cases arise in the Victorian press of self-proclaimed healers managing to kill their patients with toxic concoctions. Those same papers gave advertising space pills and ointments promising to cure all manner of ailments.

'Many persons have been destroyed by quack drugs,' wrote the eighteenth-century quack critic James Makittrick Adair, 'but dead men tell no tales.' The inclusion of mercury in particular could spell disaster, as an amateur mixing up a batch of pills containing mercury would often find most of the toxic substance ending up in half the batch, making that particular box extra harmful to whoever was unfortunate enough to purchase it. Mercury was a particular concern for physicians hoping to prevent deaths arising from the Victorian obsession with bowel movements. Browsing any number of quack medicine advertisements, you will immediately notice 'disorders of the liver' ranking highly as a curable complaint. Liver disease was a euphemism for constipation.

Bowels were an unfunny concern during the nineteenth century. For inner-city working-class families, fruit and vegetables were all too often passed up in favour of meat or cheese because vegetables simply didn't keep you feeling full during a hard day at work. The lion's share of meat went to the father or eldest son, and because food hygiene and refrigeration were all but impossible, this meat could easily contain worm eggs. If the male breadwinner hosted a tapeworm or another kind of parasite that could weaken him or stop him working, you and your family were in trouble. There were quacks who made entire careers out of telling people they were infested with parasites, and in mortal danger unless they paid for a violent purgative. Our friend Baron Spolasco was a great proponent of the laxatives-for-all approach, resulting in one woman's immediate death from a perforated stomach.

Almost every patent medicine contained some kind of laxative, mild or strong. Carter's Little Liver Pills were at one point marketed specifically to girls as a means to a beautiful complexion by invigorating the liver, or rather, purging the digestive system before it had a chance to extract nutrients from food. Another product, Bile Beans – the clue is in the name – would rid the body of what the ancient physicians called black bile, thereby making the patient as radiant and cheerful as the girls in the adverts. That outdoorsy flushed look came from running to the privy. This fixation on the bowels facilitated eating disorders and caused some deadly miscalculations, particularly in cases of dysentery and cholera. What you didn't need when voiding yourself to death was another reason to reach for the chamber pot, and even mild illnesses could be exacerbated by dehydration and long-term reliance on purgatives. But the presence of mercury in these remedies, declared or hidden, was the most immediately concerning element of all.

One tragic case in 1803 saw a 3-year-old named Thomas Clayton die a horrific death after being given Ching's Worm Lozenges. 'The benevolent proprietor,' said *The Medical Observer* three years after the child's death, 'for the purpose of concealing the composition of his nostrum from the public, has wisely specified the articles in Latin … We have thought it proper to give an English translation of these wonderful recipes.' Ching's secret ingredient was Panacea Murcurii, or mercury. Little Thomas Clayton's teeth fell out, and his body turned black, convulsing and covered in ulcers. Twenty-eight days after taking the lozenges, he died of acute mercury poisoning. When the family fought for justice, the stress caused the child's pregnant mother to miscarry, and the vendor simply skipped town. *The Medical Observer* was critical of Ching's Worm Lozenges, not for their deadly potential, but for Ching's use of pig Latin and his laughable desire to patent mercury, a very old 'cure' for worms, as his own invention. The Clayton tragedy was shrugged off. The extraordinary ability of quacks to weasel out of justice was maddening to their opponents. With the lack of legislation, there was little recourse for those who chose to dabble with patent medicine. This naturally led to many quacks claiming not to be like the others, causing no discomfort or embarrassment, or indeed death, even when their remedies were just as haphazard as any other. The number of unrecorded mishaps and tragedies owing to spurious remedies was thought to be enormous.

In 1909, some years after Thomas Holloway's death, his pills were examined by the British Medical Association and the findings were published alongside the ingredients of many popular cure-alls. *Secret Remedies – What They Cost and What They Contain* aimed to put an end to patent medicine, exposing quacks for what they were. Under each brand, the mercury content was explicitly stated. Holloway's Pills contained none. That counts in his favour – at least he wasn't knowingly poisoning people, unlike plenty of others. Over the years, various attempts were made to demystify the mighty healer's wares. Holloway's Pills were found to contain a variety of seemingly random ingredients, including ginger, soap, myrrh and turnips. Like most patent medicines, they were mainly made of aloe, a common laxative. Holloway's pills, wrote the celebrated explorer Sir Samuel Baker in the *Chemist & Druggist* in 1867, were especially good at producing a minor earthquake in the trousers. Sir Baker published what he thought was a hilarious anecdote about using Holloway's pills to hold 'Arabs in willing subjugation' while he posed as a celebrated British doctor. The insinuation was that only the primitive would believe in such a panacea.

For all the sniggering of the elite, the publication of *Secret Remedies* and books like it left a small dent in quackery at large, but business continued to boom. The law didn't help the physicians' crusade. A quack could be summonsed for pedalling pills or ointments containing little or no medicinal content, but this never meant to indicate medicinal *value*. Manufacturers of arsenic soap could be prosecuted for not containing enough of the dangerous poison, for example. Thomas Holloway's pills and ointment did not claim to contain any specific medicinal content, and were therefore free to flourish. Others, like Ching's Worm Lozenges, contained mercury and duly admitted so when applying for patents. When selling to customers concerned about ill effects, however, vendors were encouraged to deny any such ingredient, emphasising the medicine's safety. Anyone making a legal complaint could simply be informed that the patent clearly stated the ingredients, if only they had bothered to apply to read it.

Throughout the nineteenth century, business came before the safety of individuals time and time again. By 1893, the *Chemist & Druggist* magazine were convinced that big retail companies such as Boots would 'annihilate pharmacy proper' by driving down prices and selling quack medicine hard to the masses. High street stores were aiding the quacks by distributing their wares widely across Britain for prices no true doctor could compete with. Profit was the chief concern, perfectly illustrated by the *Chemist & Druggist's* own advertising pages; for all the editors' ethical concerns, the magazine was packed with fad health devices and sex aids marketed as physical therapy accessories. Well into the twentieth century, the medical profession was still fighting a slow and largely fruitless battle with the quacks.

The list of tragedy, exploitation, and fakery was a long one, but some physicians kept an eye on the press in case their names and those of their colleagues were being misused by quacks. Thomas fell into this trap almost immediately. When his advertisements started citing testimonials by a Dr Bright of Guy's Hospital, Dr Thomas Wakley, a vocal enemy of quacks and editor of *The Lancet*, protested that Holloway's Dr Bright was not the famous and respected Dr Bright of Savile Row, but in fact a man paid by Holloway himself. Surely this was proof positive that Holloway and those like him intended to mislead the public into taking bogus remedies. While we cannot know if this 'mistake' was as cynical as it appears, Thomas was fortunate to be let off the hook. Wakley urged the venerable Dr Bright to come forward and deny any involvement with Holloway's products, but Bright never did so. Presumably, a genuinely respected physician would have little time or inclination

19. This 1909 postcard shows the patent medicine trade surviving into the twentieth century.
(Verity Holloway)

to stoop to scolding patent medicine manufacturers. But Thomas was walking into risky territory.

Punch magazine knew exactly where they'd like to see quacks: in the pillory. The mighty healer, Professor Holloway, was a gold mine of comic material. *Punch* kept up their satire of Holloway throughout his career, and even after his death. His very surname became a synonym of self-puffery, a benchmark with which to measure the politicians, playwrights and would-be celebrities of Victorian London. Holloway was a 'piller of society', and if good science couldn't bring him down, perhaps mockery would.

> Mister Holloway, with that modesty which is the invariable attendant on real merit, declares that his 'Universal Ointment' will mend the legs of men and tables equally well, and be found an excellent relish for frying fish in.

Remembering Thomas's flirtatious billet-doux to Jane, mentioning wooden legs, he himself was hardly unaware of the satirical potential of his concoctions. Nevertheless ...

> Professor Holloway has shown so much vigour of imagination in his cases of 'a gentleman having recovered the use of' this that and the other, by the use of the Professor's Ointment and Pills, that we think we cannot do less than reward his ingenuity than by suggesting to him something new, in the shape of an advertisement.
>
> A gentleman recovered the use of his senses by so-and-so's pills. The patient had long been addicted to the folly of taking quack medicines, and he had resorted to every pill and ointment that came out, without deriving from any of them the smallest benefit: at length, in a fit of unusual absurdity, he tried Professor So-and-So's Pills, the effects of which were as to cause him at once to recover the use of his senses, and he has never been known from that time to take a single dose of quack medicine.

Holloway's customers were equally scorned. They were, by *Punch's* estimation, old ladies, soft in the head, and outright fools. But so what if a fool came a cropper from falling for the promises of a quack?

> Even if Holloway's Pills were good for anything at all, they might not be good for the fool's case, and the consequence might be that the world would lose a fool. No great loss this perhaps to the world, but some loss to the fool's relations and friends.

Holloway's old champion, the Earl of Aldborough, was the greatest fool of all. Not only did Holloway's Ointment cure his every ailment, but also his bank account, in return for his dignity. In one 1846 edition of *Punch*, he gets to star in his very own Puff Pantomime replete with fairies singing while he sleeps:

CHORUS OF GOOD SPIRITS
Gentle spirits treading lightly
Guard thee from terrestrial ills:
To thy pillow bringing nightly
Boxes of the welcome pills.
Ah! well-a-day, sing HOLLOWAY;

20. The Earl of Aldborough experiences the miraculous power of Holloway's Pills. *Punch*, 1846. (Verity Holloway)

Sing hey-dey, merry!
Well-a-day, sing HOLLOWAY.
Ding dong, derry.

The spirits disappear, and the Irish Earl rises. He rubs his eyes and seems refreshed.

THE EARL

What's this? Where am I? What are they about?
I dreamt that I was torn by fiends of gout;
And then methought a spirit came to cheer: − [sees a box]
It brought relief. Ha! Ha! What have we here?
There's an inscription too. What does it say?
'To him who might or would.' That means, I may ...
Within the box there's an inscription too.
'Fear not too many, but avoid too few.
Whoever would be free from earthly ills,
Will take, each night and morn, six of these pills.'
Already it is morning by the sun:
I'll trust the Genius, and I'll swallow one.

The Earl takes a pill. He gradually throws down his crutches. Tribes of fairies advance, who unroll the bandages from his legs, and he dances the *Cellarius* to the following *Chorus of Good Spirits*:

Well-a-day, HOLLOWAY! − Who would shun,
All through life terrestrial ills
Must take at the rising of the sun
One of the celebrated pills.

If Thomas knew what *Punch* were saying about him − and it's highly unlikely that he didn't, as *Punch* were still using the Earl of Aldborough as fodder long after the Earl's death, and Holloway's − he never let on that he cared. The satire did little to affect profits. *Punch* could mock the puffery of Professor Holloway, but risked a visit from the lawyers if they were to outright accuse the pills and ointment of being dangerous or knowingly useless. So imagine the editor's pleasure in 1863 when the opportunity arose to report that Professor Holloway found himself in court:

THE PANACEA PROCLAIMED!
A revelation of world-wide interest and importance has just been made in the Court of Common Pleas. It will regenerate mankind, but ruin the medical profession. This momentous disclosure is nothing less than a statement of the composition of HOLLOWAY'S OINTMENT!

Thomas had slipped up. *The Times* reported that a man named Sillen had taken Holloway to court over a £500 bill for the acquisition of a French patent for his pills and ointment. £500 was a massive sum, and Holloway had refused to pay after Sillen failed to get the patent. And why was this? *Punch* were delighted to report:

How valuable a remedy Holloway's ointment must be if it was worth Holloway's while to pay £500 for a licence to sell in France and the French colonies! For, of course, the Professor contemplated honestly paying the £500 if he got the licence and had not any legal plea for refusing to shell out; such as he turns out to have.

Sillen's application for a patent was refused on the grounds that the ointment and pills contained nothing of any medicinal value. Such a thing was no impediment in Britain, but in France the laws were stricter and secret remedies were subject to scrutiny. By refusing to pay Sillen for his failed attempt, Thomas Holloway ended up in court, forced to listen to the verdict of the French doctors who examined his wares in the lab. This included full disclosure of the ingredients, with the press standing by to take notes:

And so this, after all, is the composition of Holloway's Ointment. Butter, lard, Bordeaux turpentine, white wax, yellow wax, and nothing else! … There! No more patent or any other medicine – except Holloway's Pills and Ointment; which we now know how to make for ourselves. Professor Holloway's cat is out of the bag. Henceforth we shall all be able to cure our own diseases.

By using Sillen's failure and the cause of his failure as a defence in court, Holloway as good as admitted he was a quack. He protested that there was an ingredient the French had failed to notice (*Punch* were *certain* that wasn't a lie) but the whole episode was a farce. The only saving grace was that readers of *The Times* were likely able to afford physicians, and those of *Punch* were already wise to quackery. As hilarious as it was to see Holloway in the dock, the staff of *Punch* knew little would come of the case. As the decades passed, their war on quackery became more serious, even emotional: a cartoon from 1893 depicts a mountebank with a drummer boy plying his trade while a nearby policeman does nothing to stop him. The *Punch* mascot looks on with uncharacteristic solemnity. 'Really, ordinary newspapers ought to leave medical science alone,' one editorial says on the subject of 'puff pieces' and fictional testimonials filling the pages of household periodicals all over the country. Fools the customers might be, but the blame lay at the feet of the advertisers as much as the quacks themselves.

If the law wasn't going to help the fight against quacks, laughter was the next best thing. William Makepeace Thackeray, sharp-clawed satirist and author of *Vanity Fair*, was no lover of those who made their money from the credulity of others:

> There are bullies pushing about, bucks ogling the women, knaves picking pockets, policemen on the look-out, quacks (OTHER quacks, plague take them!) bawling in front of their booths ... Let us have at them, dear friends, with might and main. Some there are, and very successful too, mere quacks and fools: and it was to combat and expose such as those, no doubt, that Laughter was made.

Thackeray was a believer in ridicule as antidote. As a contributor to *Punch*, he was well aware of the magazine's long-running siege on

Thomas Holloway and his ilk, so when the author came unexpectedly face to face with the professor in 1851, the result was predictably cringeworthy.

The Great Exhibition at the Crystal Palace was the first international exhibition of manufactured products, showcasing inventive ingenuity from all over the British Empire. Thomas, naturally, visited the exhibition, perhaps with a view to networking with the great and good. He met up with George Sala, a journalist and associate of Edmund Yates, who would later dance his way around Holloway's shop on the Strand. Sala was known (and tittered at) for his bombastic writing style in *The Daily Telegraph*, but he was nonetheless an engaging character with plenty of connections. Thomas asked Sala to introduce him to Thackeray; something that would make him 'supremely happy'. Sala recollected the incident years later:

> I hesitated at first; but, fancying that I discerned a benevolent twinkle beneath the great man's spectacles, I took heart of grace and did the 'Professor's' bidding. It is no secret to those who really knew the illustrious William Makepiece [*sic*] that he could say upon occasion things which made you intensely uncomfortable.

Before introductions could be formally made, the famous novelist mistook Holloway for a high-ranking military man and greeted him cordially until realizing his error. 'Oh well, I must have made a natural mistake, for you, too, must have killed your thousands!' He then made the Professor a very low and stiff bow, and said, 'I hope, sir, that you will live longer than your patients.'

Accounts of the snub's wording vary, but Sala was undoubtedly relieved when other acquaintances intervened and cleared the air:

> About half an hour afterwards I met Mr Holloway ... just as he was departing, and he delivered himself of this remarkable utterance, 'That Mr Thackeray may think himself a very clever man; but I fancy that I could buy him up, ten times over.' The 'Professor's'

good nature, however, speedily reasserted itself, and shaking my hand cordially, he said: 'Good-by, Sir, I am very much obliged to you; and if you ever start a periodical I shall be happy to give you a half-page advertisement.'

As plenty of his fellow nouveau riche had already discovered, Thomas found that money wasn't necessarily a ticket into Victorian high circles.

And then there was Dickens. Dickens, as we've already seen, found Holloway's poster campaign suffocating, but there were other ways for astute businessmen to insert themselves into the public's consciousness. *Punch's* aforementioned takedown of the Earl of Aldborough in their pantomime sketch was a comment on the product placement that had become hard to avoid in Victorian light entertainment. Businesses could slip playwrights and authors a fee in return for featuring their product in their work, and the practice had become commonplace enough for theatregoers to begin to find this annoying. However, a nod from a prominent author in one of the wildly popular serialised novels of the day could be a boon for any company. Anyone looking to boost their profile into the stratosphere would naturally be eyeing Dickens, and after Holloway's death in 1883, several reports surfaced of Holloway doing just that. Society gossip Edmund Yates published his own recollection:

> The announcement of the death of Mr Holloway – 'Professor' Holloway he used to call himself – will bring back many memories to the middle-aged. Of the long narrow shop close by Temple Bar, on the spot where the Law Courts now stand, with its long row of seated assistants all engaged in rolling pills or spreading ointment; and the suite of rooms above, crammed with piles of journals from all parts of the world, to which gratuitous reference was permitted; of the lists of wonderful cures of 'bad legs of many years' standing', as the advertisement ran; and of his great decoy-duck, a peer, the Earl of Aldborough, who published a testimonial to the worth of

the famous pills. The 'bad leg', or something else, has carried Lord Aldborough off now, and the title is extinct.

He was a shrewd amusing man, this same 'Professor', and was very daring. He once enclosed a cheque for a thousand pounds in a letter to Charles Dickens, which he placed at Dickens's disposal, on condition that one line of complimentary reference to Holloway's cures should appear in the book which Dickens was then publishing in monthly numbers. The bearer waited for an answer. 'What did you do?' I asked Dickens. 'Do!' he cried; 'I put the cheque back into the letter and sent it down to the messenger, saying that was all the answer I had to send!'

Another version of the story has Thackeray suggesting Dickens take the money and kill a character with a dose of Holloway's Pills. But did it happen? Yates was a smirking, cigar-sucking rogue, later sentenced to four months' imprisonment for unrelated defamatory libel, and had already been expelled from The Garrick Club by Thackeray for another unfair article. Both Dickens and Holloway were dead by the time the article was published, and Dickens himself isn't known to have written any similar recollection. Yates's 'playful anecdotes' are to be treated with scepticism, but there's a faint ring of truth in the way he paints Holloway's advertising guile, and the annoyance it caused. It was said that 'millions who have never heard of Napoleon … have heard of Holloway,' a deliberate nod to the international conquest (barring France) of his pills and ointment. Even if untrue, the anecdote only goes to prove the immensity of Holloway's reach. This cultural awareness of Holloway had positive connotations as well as negative, sometimes from peculiar sources. Karl Marx ridiculed an opponent's love of the sound of his own voice by saying there was as much chance as escaping him as escaping Holloway's adverts. In an 1876 speech, Prime Minister Gladstone compared the efficacy of his policies to the purifying powers of Holloway's Pills, though one has to question his wisdom. There would always be those who swore by quack medicine, as there are now. *Punch* regularly received letters from readers admonishing

21. Quacks were a useful satirical device for cartoonists. Prime Minister Gladstone is shown here drumming up business like a travelling swindler. Chromolithograph by T. Merry, 1889.
(Wellcome Library, London)

them for their anti-homeopathy views – such letters received short shrift. But it goes to show the leviathan of Holloway's advertising drowned out any criticism of his products.

Money was coming in fast. Thomas made some sensible decisions on the stock market and continued to live without extravagance, taking watered-down wine at dinner and working every day, including Christmas. He moved with his extended family to Tittenhurst Park, a handsome Georgian manor house between Sunninghill and Sunningdale in the fashionable county of Berkshire. The house would later belong to John Lennon and feature on the sleeve of *Hey Jude*. With 72 acres of land, it was the sort of house one could raise a large family in, though Thomas and Jane never did. Thomas preferred dogs, anyway. And his existing family were once again causing problems. Thomas's sister Caroline had married a modestly wealthy man who left her a widow aged fifty. At first, Thomas was glad to do his brotherly duty, helping Caroline and her sons with rent and bills, as well as letting Jane send gifts of small household items. He refused to keep count of the cheques he sent her, telling Caroline that if she tried to keep any accounts in order to pay him back, he would simply refuse to look at them. Caroline and her children enjoyed a comfortable enough existence, with seaside holidays at Uncle Thomas's behest. However, liberties were taken.

William 'Willie' Henry Young, Caroline's youngest son, had long dreamt of the stage. He had hitherto been studying law on Thomas's patronage, but when law proved tedious, Willie dropped his studies. Rumour spread that Willie was using his newfound legal knowledge to indulge in dubious business practices, and so Thomas used his contacts to find Willie a respectable position as a bank clerk. But this, too, was boring, and Willie started taking unauthorised holidays, complaining of a weak chest. Thomas again stuck his neck out for his nephew, promising his employers that a good dose of Margate air would soon have Willie back in the office – all at his expense. A weak chest didn't stop Willie marrying and having five children during this time (indeed, he married twice more and lived until 1920), and with his uncle funding his flaky lifestyle, Willie saw no reason not to pursue his dreams of theatrical fame in London's theatre district. Cheeky letters started arriving at Tittenhurst, and Thomas dealt with them accordingly.

'Why you send me your railway ticket, I know not ... Now as regards your holidays this must be a matter that concerns you – it does not me.'

And the following day: 'I can give you no advice as to what course you should pursue – you know how things stand.'

When Thomas repeatedly refused to support Willie's wife and children while he auditioned for parts, Willie dropped his job at the bank to tread the boards anyway. Thomas began receiving desperate letters from Willie's wife. Thomas regarded Willie's actions as little more than extortion. Thomas's young brother-in-law, George Martin, wrote on his behalf:

My dear Georgiana – your two last letters have been received by your uncle. As he told you in his last he should not write to you again. I am doing so to let you know his resolve concerning you.

Your husband has gone away. He must be brought back and must support you as best he can. If you or some friend were to write to Miss Swanborough at the Strand Theatre acquainting her that your husband had gone away and left you perfectly destitute & had only send you 10/- since he left & beg of her to have him dismissed that he may return home, it would bring him back.

It is of no use for him to talk about not being desirous to shew himself in London – he has reduced himself & you now & forever to a position scarcely above that of a labourer & which you and he must realise. We all pity you from our hearts – but your uncle [will] give you no more money – not one shilling, no matter how great your distress may be – should you even have to go into the Union – Do not then for a moment fancy that your prayers – or your distress – will have any effect upon him – so take your measures accordingly.

I desire that you understand that your uncle would have been most willing to have assisted you & your children – had your wretched & most worthless husband instead of leaving you had sought employment of some kind or other but to go away believing that his uncle would support you he will find to your sorrow that he will do nothing of the kind.

Not as hard-hearted as he wished to appear, Thomas did in fact pay Georgiana's rent and taxes, and made sure she had food. He insisted that her husband's actions had in no way diminished his regard for her. As in the case of Mister Rough and his ill-spent wages, Thomas hated seeing men's families suffering for their poor decisions. Charity, he said, had a way of demeaning those who received it. Easy enough for a man sitting on a fortune to say, but in Willie's case, tough love mostly did the trick. He returned to his family and opened a butcher's shop. Some years later, he appeared on stage at the Royal Court Theatre alongside his daughter.

In the mid-1860s, Thomas was in danger of resembling the miserly stereotype of the cunning quack with his ill-gotten gains. Hundreds of testimonials – which Thomas swore were genuine – assured him his products were doing some good in the world, even if that good came only from the placebo effect. Whether Thomas was feeling the nip of conscience or not, we cannot know. Perhaps *Punch* and Thackeray had touched a nerve. But, in 1864, he resolved to put his profits into good causes. First, he attempted to place a large donation to his native Devonport, but the offer was refused, perhaps owing to his occupation. Thomas needed a direction. He found one in the form of George Peabody, the American philanthropist whose contribution to society would earn him a Westminster Abbey funeral. In an anonymous open letter published in Britain's foremost architectural magazine, *The Builder*, Thomas stated he wished to fund a project for the greatest public good; something useful for people who may not be eligible for charity, but not wealthy either.

He was having difficulty arriving at such a scheme, and invited public opinion, though in truth, Thomas harboured fledgling ideas of his own. When the radical social reformer Lord Shaftesbury was privately consulted it became clear what group of people Thomas felt moved to aid – a most unusual choice for a purveyor of quack medicine.

Chapter 9

'Good God; in England, in this country?'

Dufor ing the 1830s, John Perceval, the son of the only British Prime Minister to be assassinated, experienced a mental breakdown. He was confined to two of the country's most prestigious private asylums – Ticehurst House and Brislington House – for a total of eighteen months. In 1840, Perceval was sufficiently recovered to publish a memoir of his ordeal – *A Narrative of The Treatment Experienced by a Gentleman, During a State of Mental Derangement* – with the aim of revealing to the public the abuses and humiliations the mentally ill suffered at the hands of those employed to care for them.

Perceval's 'derangement' (his own word) was religious in nature, an obsessive belief that he was moved by the Holy Spirit, fed by the trauma of his father's death on the steps of the Houses of Parliament. After dropping university to join a Scottish sect of Evangelicals who claimed to speak in tongues and perform miracles, Perceval contracted venereal disease from a prostitute, necessitating a dose of mercury. His behaviour became so erratic that his family saw no other option than to send him to an asylum. He wrote lucidly of his experiences there; his feelings of betrayal by his family, the disrespect from doctors and staff, and their inhumane efforts to keep him quiet and compliant instead of attempting to treat his delusions. Perceval quickly found that, as a lunatic, the law would not come to his aid. He believed that the treatment of a gentleman lunatic was especially cruel; a fall from a position of respect and dignity that could never be fully regained. Having no more power to wield, he turned to the only protest available to him: silence.

> From that [first] moment to the end of my confinement, men acted
> as though my body, soul, and spirit were fairly given up to their
> control, to work their mischief and folly upon. My silence, I suppose,
> gave consent. I mean, that I was never told, such and such things
> we are going to do; we think it is advisable to administer such
> and such medicine, in this or that manner; I was never asked, Do
> you want any thing? Do you wish for, or prefer, any thing? Have
> you any objection to this or to that? I was fastened down in bed;
> a meager diet was ordered for me; this and medicine forced down
> my throat, or in the contrary direction; my will, my wishes, my
> repugnances, my habits, my delicacy, my inclinations, my necessities,
> were not once consulted, I may say, thought of.

Perceval felt reduced to the status of an animal. And yet he was
an inmate of two of the finest institutions available to his class;
beautiful country houses with lush grounds. For the poor, the
situation was more desperate. Before the establishment of public
asylums in the mid-Victorian period, many inmates of workhouses
were there as a result of mental illness – their own, or a family
member's. Even after the provision of public institutions, there are
cases of the mentally ill being forced to throw themselves on the
mercy of the workhouse. Considered the absolute last resort, fear
of the workhouse ran deep. Families would be separated according
to gender, their individuality stripped from them with a regime
of hard physical work, uncomfortable lodging, and food barely
nutritious enough to keep them alive. In extreme cases, such as an
incident at Andover Workhouse in 1845, starving inmates resorted
to sucking the marrow from discarded bones.

Public asylums were a necessary pressure valve for overcrowded
prisons and workhouses. Everyone has heard of London's 'Bedlam'
or Bethlem Asylum – a name that eventually became a byword
for chaos. Bethlem began its long history as a priory in 1247,
approximately where Liverpool Street Station stands today. As a
hospital for psychiatric purposes, Bethlem has existed for 600 years,
moving to various new sites around the capital. At the beginning

22. Hogarth's *The Rake's Progress; scene at Bedlam.* Engraving by T. Cook, after William
Hogarth. Published 1796.
(Wellcome Library, London)

of the nineteenth century, Bethlem was home to a broad spectrum
of 'lunatic', from battle-traumatised soldiers to the newly created
category of the criminally insane. Many patients were permanent
residents, housed like prisoners to keep them off the streets, with
no attempt to treat their maladies.

Urbane Metcalf, a travelling salesman, survived Bethlem to tell
the tale. Writing in 1818, he reported that doctors and orderlies
were openly corrupt, pitting the patients against each other for
entertainment, squandering money, and showing no interest
whatsoever in curing their charges beyond cursory bloodletting
and purges. Deaths were hushed up.

> Cruelty is common to them all; villainy is common to them all; in short every thing is common but virtue, which is so uncommon they take care to lock it up as a rarity. Like other establishments this appears to be erected too much for the purpose of making lucrative places; the apartments appropriated to the use of the officers are elegant in the extreme.

This juxtaposition of profit and useless treatment brings to mind the business practices of quacks. Metcalf was placed on 'the long list', diagnosed as incurable. The long list was wielded as a threat to patients unwilling to cooperate – they would find themselves infinitely detained.

> Coles, a patient of Blackburn's, one day, for refusing to take his physic [a purgative], was by Blackburn and Rodbird beat and dashed violently against the wall several times, in the presence of the steward, though from the general tenor of this man's conduct it is probable a little persuasion would have been sufficient to induce him to take the medicine quietly, Coles is since put upon the long list.

Unsurprisingly, the Bethlem orderlies branded Metcalf a troublemaker. He was confined to a solitary room and went on to escape from the hospital in 1806. Twice he was sent back, but when his 1818 pamphlet garnered attention from the public and politicians, Metcalf won his release by the power of publicity. The staff were probably glad to see him go.

The Victorian dichotomy of the deserving and undeserving poor was deeply rooted. In a time before social security, to fall on hard times could mean utter ruin, and the blame could easily be laid at the feet of the victims. 'Madness', it was said, could be brought about by an excess of drink, sexual indulgence, or even fabricated entirely – all the fault of the individual. Bethlem's notoriety did nothing to assuage public dislike of the mad. Beggars pretending to be mad for sympathy appear in slang dictionaries as 'Abraham-men', after

Bethlem's Abraham ward. In 1675, the Bethlem governors issued a statement warning the public that these men were fraudulently claiming to be inmates set free for a day, proceeding to rob and intimidate their way around town. Abraham Men survived in slang long into the Victorian age. As for mad women, one of the nineteenth century's most enduring ballads, *Crazy Jane*, tells of a jilted lover driven out of her wits:

> *Why, fair maid, in ev'ry feature,*
> *Are such signs of fear express'd?*
> *Can a wandering wretched creature,*
> *With such terrors fill thy breast?*
> *Do my frenzied looks alarm thee?*
> *Trust me, sweet, thy fears are vain;*
> *Not for kingdoms would I harm thee;*
> *Shun not then poor Crazy Jane.*
>
> *Dost thou weep to see my anguish?*
> *Mark me, and avoid my woe,*
> *When men flatter, sigh and languish,*
> *Think them false – I found them so.*
> *For I lov'd – Oh, so sincerely,*
> *None could ever love again,*
> *But the youth I lov'd so dearly,*
> *Stole the wits of Crazy Jane.*

The wild-eyed figure of Crazy Jane was adapted into art and poetry repeatedly throughout the century, most notably by Richard Dadd, the fairy artist confined to Bethlem after killing his father during a breakdown. The note of sympathy running through the ballad is less to do with Jane's mental state than its supposed cause, her sexual undoing: 'He was false – and I undone.' Crazy Jane loses her mind, but more importantly, her respectability. She is turned into a figure of curiosity and pity, living on the edge of the community. Whatever the cause, mad was not a respectable thing to be.

Dignity, and the loss of it, features highly in contemporary criticisms of asylums, whether public or private. John Perceval's complaints about his asylum experience tended to dwell on loss of gentlemanly dignity, being forced to take orders from 'vulgar persons' he deemed socially beneath him, with no hope of contesting their decisions in a court of law. In his account, a reader can glean hints of the pleasure the staff gained from their position of power over a well-born gentleman. For Urbane Metcalf, his experience in Bethlem was comparable to slavery. For both men, the consensus seemed clear: lunatics, if not branded outright incurable, were simply not deserving of the effort required to find a cure or even relieve their symptoms. Releasing the patient's family of the burden of care, however, was a lucrative business – one that would always attract villains.

As Metcalf himself wrote: 'Good God; in England, in this country?' Many were outraged, but reform of mental healthcare was almost as slow as that of the regulation of patent medicine. Following his recovery, Perceval formed the Alleged Lunatic's Friend Society in 1845, together with a small group of ex-inmates, their relatives, and supporters. The aims of the society were to protect people from wrongful confinement or cruelty, and to bring about reform of the law to give patients back a measure of autonomy. The society had but a few high-ranking supporters. By the time Thomas Holloway toyed with thoughts of philanthropy, Anthony Ashley-Cooper, 7th Earl of Shaftesbury, had made it his life's work to advocate for the humane treatment of society's least fortunate members: child labourers, miners, and those considered lunatics. The average pauper asylum was 'a mere place for dying', he argued, packed with alcoholics, those born with learning disabilities (known then as 'naturals'), homosexuals, unwed mothers, the depressed, and the traumatised. With no understanding of how to treat any of these people, asylums were little more than holding pens; a shame on a Christian nation. Societies like Perceval's could only do so much. The government had to get involved.

Shaftesbury campaigned for decades to improve conditions. His radical notion that the mentally ill deserved humane treatment was initially met with scorn, but as the century rolled on, attitudes were progressing towards something more hopeful. Colney Hatch, another London pauper asylum, had been opened in 1851 by Prince Albert. A guidebook was proudly issued to visitors of the Crystal Palace, where Thomas Holloway had been on the receiving end of Thackeray's acid. Philanthropists, it said, would find the endeavour of particular interest.

Colney Hatch was welcomed as a new kind of asylum. Built in the Italian style with space for a thousand patients, it boasted an onsite bakery, laundry, workrooms, farmhouses, a chapel for up to 400 faithful, and even a ballroom. Patients were permitted to keep canaries – indeed, they bred them in a designated building on the grounds, showing remarkable forward thinking as far as therapy was

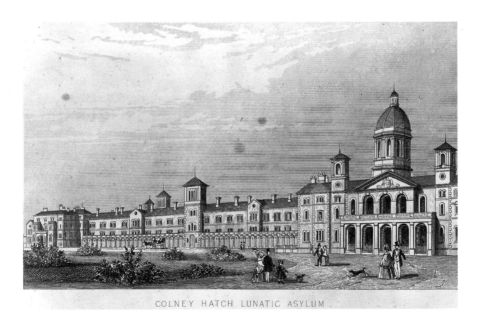

COLNEY HATCH LUNATIC ASYLUM

23. Colney Hatch was meant to be an asylum in the truest sense of the word. Colney Hatch Lunatic Asylum, Southgate, Middlesex: panoramic view. Engraving, Anon. (Wellcome Library, London)

concerned. With its own gasworks and direct railway supply routes, Colney Hatch would hopefully avoid the curse of institutions before it: inescapable cold, damp, and stale air, contributing to infectious diseases and general sickliness. Modern and humane were the watchwords of this new establishment. Perhaps Thomas Holloway picked up a copy of the guidebook in 1851. If he had paid attention over the following years, he may have heard about the asylum's swift decline. Built in a hurry, small oversights snowballed into serious problems. The asphalt lining the interior walls collected foul smells. The windows wouldn't open more than an inch. Worse, for the neighbours, the asylum's sewage leaked into the local water supply. The General Board of Health was summoned to inspect the resulting cesspool, but not before the inevitable outbreaks of dysentery and typhoid. Six miles of corridors, once a source of pride, became dark, smelly, and nightmarish. Like Bedlam before it, Colney Hatch was the butt of music hall jokes; the hospital's very name became a term of abuse. The project was a bitter failure.

The Earl of Shaftesbury received a cordial letter from one Thomas Holloway in 1864. Shaftesbury was a year younger than Thomas, but his rather grim physiognomy made him appear older. Like Thomas, Shaftesbury had been lampooned in the press, though for opposite reasons. He was an easy target, with his zeal for reform comically at odds with his dour face. What Shaftesbury thought of Holloway's Pills and Ointment is unknown, but the letter clearly impressed him, and Holloway was duly invited to the Earl's Grosvenor Square accommodation to discuss Thomas's fortune and the spending of it. Despite being born into privilege, Shaftesbury had weathered a childhood of neglect and was largely raised by one of the household's maids, Maria Millis. It was Millis who introduced him to the Evangelical faith and the sense of social responsibility that came with it. Shaftesbury had spent more than half a century campaigning on behalf of the poor, of working children, and the insane, but all his attempts at raising funds for an institution of his own had failed. Despite his severe appearance, the Earl was an impressive orator whose speeches filled halls, and Thomas had taken time out of his manic work schedule to see him speak on the subject of asylums and the plight of those inside. As Chairman of the Commissioners in Lunacy, the first parliamentary body set up to deal with the abuses of the asylums, Shaftesbury had seen in person the indignities awaiting the sick, whether rich or poor. In his diary, a year before John Perceval formed the Alleged Lunatic's Friend Society, Shaftesbury wrote of his horror at visiting a private asylum in Peckham:

> What a lesson! How small the interval – a hair's breadth! – between reason and madness. A sight, too, to stir apprehension in one's own mind. I am visiting in authority today. I may be visited by authority tomorrow. God be praised there are any visitations at all; time was when such care was unknown. What an awful condition that of a lunatic! His words are generally disbelieved, and his most innocent

24. Anthony Ashley Cooper, 7th Earl of Shaftesbury. Photograph by Lock & Whitfield. (Wellcome Library, London)

peculiarities perverted … Thus we too readily get him in, and too
sluggishly get him out, and yet what a destiny!

The middle classes, he and Holloway agreed, were in a difficult
position. With expensive private institutions at one end of the
spectrum and the likes of Bethlem at the other, the middle classes
were somewhat hard to deal with. Despite being comfortably off,
these families frequently struggled to afford the special diets and
country air physicians prescribed for melancholy daughters and
troubled sons. For more serious conditions, a public asylum was
out of the question – even if they qualified, the humiliation would
have been unconscionable – and private ones were beyond reach,
especially as the illness itself often stopped the individual from
bringing money into the household. Most people in this position were
forced to rely on charity. Middle-class life could be precarious, as
well Thomas knew from his time inside Whitecross Prison. Largely
untreatable, mental illness all too often led to penury for entire
families. Thomas listened to the horrors described by Shaftesbury
and looked at his own good fortune, financial and otherwise. Both
men saw an opportunity to take this gap in care and fill it with
something that actually worked. With better planning and attention
to detail, Colney Hatch may have lived up to its high aims. With
more money, such failures could be avoided.

Over the following years, a plan was formulated. Thomas
would put his name to a sanatorium. This sanatorium was to be
a refuge, not for the incurable, but for those who would do well
with good surroundings and moral occupation. The decision not
to use the word 'asylum' reveals plenty about Thomas's intentions.
In America, the word 'sanatorium' was 'asylum's' polite equivalent.
Thomas most likely wanted to cast a veneer of respectability over
his establishment, separating it from the grim past. Perhaps, too,
he wished to imply the validity of invisible illness – in Europe,
sanatoriums were associated with long-term physical illnesses, such
as tuberculosis. Not only did it imply that mental illness was to be

treated with the same gravity as physical disease, but also optimism: at a sanatorium, there was a chance to be cured.

Thomas's meetings with the Earl of Shaftesbury caught the attention of higher powers. To his surprise, a letter arrived at Tittenhurst – from the Prime Minister's wife. Catherine Gladstone requested 'the pleasure and the advantage of a little conversation' with Mister Holloway, whose 'noble schemes and a desire to do good for suffering humanity' had piqued her husband's deep interest. A meeting between Thomas and the Gladstones took place on 17 July 1873. Catherine hoped it was not too forward of her to offer her own input to the project, as she herself had some experience of the running of convalescent homes. Indeed it was not, and besides, she was being modest. Catherine's biographers have since celebrated the dynamic, untidy woman's 'genius' for social change, taking energetic interest in concerns for the less fortunate, with little patience for the political skullduggery that so often hindered meaningful change. In a private project such as this, ambitions were limited only by funds. Thomas returned home that night full of fervor.

Holloway Sanatorium would be a peaceful place of recovery for skilled middle-class individuals whose occupation had been endangered by their health – scholars, artists, doctors, lawyers, and the like. Women, too, would be catered for, as well as those on the lower income end of the spectrum, subsidised by the fees of the wealthier patients. Past mistakes had to be avoided. The utmost care was to be taken in planning and building such an institution. Spending would be lavish. After all, it would bear the Holloway name.

A tour of existing asylums was plotted out. Thomas employed his young brother-in-law George Martin as his agent, and together they travelled England and America, taking in the finest institutions the world had to offer at Thomas's usual breakneck speed. They concluded that a lighter approach was needed; something more akin to one of the British water-cure resorts Thomas himself had been known to use in the past, where treatment was combined with leisure. Existing asylums, consciously or otherwise, had an air of punishment about them. Thomas was envisioning something more inviting, even holiday-like, close to his own home in pretty, green Sunninghill. One prevailing modern stereotype of the Victorian asylum is eerie isolation, keeping patients away from the public like a dirty secret. Many surviving English asylums have since had towns develop around them, but were originally situated in semi-rural areas in keeping with the belief that greenery was good for the soul. The Commissioners in Lunacy specifically recommended an asylum should be placed on elevated ground and should command cheerful prospects, with land sufficient to afford outdoor employment for males, exercise for all patients, and to protect them from being overlooked or disturbed by strangers. It's no accident that some of these nineteenth-century institutions have since been turned into golf clubs or sought-after gated communities. The eminently lush and leafy Virginia Water was decided on as the perfect spot. Thomas and George Martin devised a competition for architects to present their prospective plans.

The winner would have to be someone extraordinary. On returning from their inspirational travels – fifteen countries in three weeks! – Thomas remarked that nothing he had seen was worth emulating, as 'the class of architects to whom such buildings have been trusted are not men possessed of great ability.' He was a particular and exacting man, already making enquiries as to whether tea and coffee were suitable beverages for people prone to fits of nervousness, and how to elegantly deal with dirty linen. This was not simply a method of putting his money to use – this project, from the start, was personal.

A great deal of theorizing was done during the nineteenth century as to aesthetics and their effect upon the mind. William Morris, the great socialist and artist, famously said that no one should have anything in their home that was not beautiful or useful. The Arts and Crafts movement Morris was driving was partly inspired by theories of Neo-Gothicism. John Ruskin, the most influential art critic of the period, wished for Neo-Gothic to bring the aesthetic purity of the medieval age up to date, to fight the poison of materialism and mechanization that the Industrial Revolution had brought with it. For Ruskin, the ideal building should aspire to seven 'Lamps', including the truthful quality of traditional handcrafting, the joy of creativity, and aspiration towards God and the sublime quality of nature that had stirred the Romantic poets. The airiness of Gothic buildings could be said to be a reaction against the cramped conditions of the expanding cities where workers were denied the dignity of their once-revered status as craftsmen and artisans. Neo-Gothic aimed to bring back light, space, and colour. Beauty, after all, was good for the soul, and if public buildings could embody beauty and aspiration, all men and women would benefit. No one was better suited to advise on this than Edward Welby Pugin, one of the century's finest architects, and champion of the Neo-Gothic.

Pugin had tragic personal experience of the asylum system. As a boy in 1852, he accompanied his father Augustus – himself a celebrated architect – on a railway journey to London. By the time the pair reached their destination, Augustus was unable to recognise anyone or sensibly communicate. He was sent to Bethlem, then situated opposite St George's Cathedral – one of his own buildings. There was public outcry that a man as gifted as he should come to such a fate, but Augustus swiftly deteriorated and died later that year. Thomas Holloway made contact with Edward Welby Pugin in the 1870s, seeking his advice on the sanatorium project. Although the response has since been lost, Thomas later made reference to a suggestion 'a great man' had made to him. Instead of an Italian style building as Colney Hatch had been, this great man advised something more Gothic, in the grand old Flemish style. Thomas remembered his youth in France and Belgium; in particular the striking Cloth Hall he had admired in Ypres, with its reaching spires and delicate filigree decorations. It was a geometrical building, suggesting the orderliness appropriate for an asylum, with archways and tall windows welcoming in plenty of optimistic light. Thomas had this ideal in mind when he and George Martin awaited the results of the competition.

Enter William Henry Crossland. Like Holloway, Crossland came from relative obscurity. Born in Huddersfield, his early life has proved hard to pin down for many researchers. Self-described poet and hack Sir John Betjeman wrote, 'Holloway's architect, Crossland, seems to have been a likeable, exuberant person, but exactly where and when he was born and where and when he died, and whether he married and had children, I cannot discover.' Crossland's buildings, however, left a lasting impression on all who saw them: 'They have to be seen to be believed, and once seen they haunt the mind like a recurring and exalting dream.' The Yorkshireman certainly had the Gothic flair Thomas was looking for. One of his previous projects, Rochdale Town Hall, was practically a castle, complete with flying buttresses, spiral staircases, and stone lions bearing coats of arms between their paws. Crossland was only thirty-eight when Thomas Holloway commissioned him to plan his sanatorium. The collaboration would make his name.

This account was probably written by Crossland himself, and was published in newspapers across the globe:

> Commenced some seven years ago by Mr Thomas Holloway, the Sanatorium for Curable Cases of Mental Disease was originally intended by the founder as a gift to the nation, perfect and complete as it stood. Mr Holloway has resolved not only to make a gift of the building, but to invest an additional £50,000 as an endowment, which will raise the cost of the whole foundation to £350,000. The purpose for which it is designed is clearly defined by the founder to be the succour of persons of the middle-class afflicted with mental disease. In selecting this object he has been guided by the consideration that rich people so unfortunate as to suffer from mental disease need no monetary assistance; and the poor in a similar mental condition are already cared for in public asylums. Put

broadly, the scope of the Holloway Sanatorium includes the doctor, lawyer, artist, clerk or any professional bread-winner whose work cannot, like an ordinary business, be carried on by deputy, and whose income ceases absolutely when he is unable to work. This definition has not been arrived at without due care and ample investigation. Mr George Martin, at the instance of Mr Holloway, and sometimes accompanying him, has visited the principal establishments for the cure of mental disease in Europe and America, and the opinion has been gradually formed that many curable cases among the middle class are allowed to become uncurable from lack of means or opportunity to secure proper treatment. Slight cerebal attacks, if dealt with promptly, may, it is well known, be cured, and a recurrence of them guarded against with considerable success, while if neglected they increase in frequency, until the patient becomes entirely incapacitated from pursuing his calling. It is simply as a curative institution that the handsome structure at Virginia Water has been founded, one of the conditions being that no patient will be allowed to remain more than twelve months.

The Commissioners of Lunacy were delighted with Thomas's model building, and he continued to seek their advice. It was agreed that Crossland's original plans would need modification. Sadly the original has not survived. The sanatorium, Thomas was determined, would be world class. He insisted on being involved in even the tiniest of details, seeking out medical professionals to quiz on the minutiae. How many single rooms would require fireplaces? Would window shutters be advisable? How best to encourage patients to socialise? Craftsmen and wholesalers found themselves on the receiving end of Thomas's sharp business sense. 'Sir,' he wrote to one such wholesaler, 'I have your invoices and must say the price you charge for bedsteads astonishes me beyond measure.' His towel racks simply would not do for the middle-class lunatic, either, and the less said about the drawer handles, the better. Every detail had to supersede the standards of existing asylums everywhere. As Thomas wrote in 1871, when the sanatorium was still a dream: 'If people will only take pains – & which is something I generally do

THE HOLLOWAY SANATORIUM AT VIRGINIA WATER.

25. Holloway Sanatorium, in all its Gothic glory.
(Wellcome Library, London)

when I take any thing in hand – they will find there is something to be learned everywhere.'

As Crossland discovered, Thomas wasn't the easiest of men to please. He tended to take it upon himself to oversee the workmen, firing off tart letters to their superiors. 'Take away the tiles,' he ordered one Mister Smitherman. 'Failing this I will have the tiles laid by competent persons, not by you, and charge you with their labour.' Young workmen were the worst, larking about and wasting time. No man under twenty-five would therefore be permitted to work on the project. Sourcing bricks was too slow a task, so Thomas bought his own brickworks. Crossland was not exempt from Thomas's somewhat controlling nature. As a man used to being in charge, Thomas was never one to leave decisions to others. 'The fastening of [the] windows appears to me to be of the utmost importance,' he wrote to Crossland in October 1874. 'For if you have not got the right kind of thing, the ingenuity of a madman will enable him to open it, and so get out and break his neck.' Crossland seems to have taken this backseat driving with patience and obedience. Thomas was never prone to gushing praise, so when he wrote to his long-suffering architect with encouragement, we can be sure he meant it: 'You are sowing the seed now to reap hereafter a golden harvest.' In the future, he promised, when people wanted to see a model of the perfect sanatorium, everyone would recommend Mister William Crossland's marvelous work at Virginia Water. And that perfect sanatorium would bear the Holloway name.

George Martin was also proving an invaluable ally. Martin had a natural eye for detail, and despite starting his working life as a seafaring man, he possessed a firm understanding of the theories of aesthetics and the mind. He and Thomas grew so close over their shared vision, the younger man would ultimately go on to adopt the Holloway surname as his own.

Dominated by the idea that a cultivated person whose mind is affected will never be cured if surrounded by vulgar idiots or grim accessories, Mr Martin has endeavored to introduce as many objects as possible to awake and stimulate the trained intelligence for the moment over-strained. In the smaller but still ample parlours and living rooms the same idea of cheerfulness and suggestiveness is carried out. It is endeavored above all things to avoid leaving a dimmed intelligence opposite to a blank wall.

Crossland's press release was overly modest. The interior was breathtaking. Part Moorish palace, part medieval hall, with cavernous communal rooms and grand staircases, the sanatorium was more hotel than hospital. There were libraries in both the male and female wings, a Turkish bath with a steam room, and a terrace for patients to take the air, looking out on to green countryside. One could choose to play bowls, or cricket, or tennis, and in the winter, the tennis courts were flooded for ice skating. In the vaulted dining room, patients were treated as honoured guests with tables set just as they would be in any respectable restaurant. Indoor ferns flourished in the good light. And of course, all over the building, were the initials of Thomas and Jane, reminding all who walked beneath the Gothic arches to whom they owed this opulence. The Holloway coat of arms was largely artistic licence – not many sons of Cornish publicans had noble heritage – but who was likely to notice a little white lie amongst all this beauty? Few could deny the sanatorium was an astonishing gift to the nation. Did Thomas stand back to look at this enormous spectacle and wonder how he had got here?

A typical day for a patient at Holloway Sanatorium meant three things: order, security, and therapy. Before even entering as a patient, middle-class propriety had to be preserved. Therefore, the concerned families of prospective patients were invited to send their enquiries to medical superintendent Doctor Rees Philips, Virginia Water, Chertsey, thus avoiding any mention of asylums or sanatoriums on the envelope. On top of this, entry was initially voluntary. Doctor Rees Phillips, who had plenty of experience caring for the middle classes, knew the psychological effect of involuntary detainment and the associated stigma. Even if the treatment did the patient good, families at home could well expect to become the subject of gossip, and as most Holloway patients came from the respectable communities of London and other major cities, chatter was a major concern. In time, Holloway Sanatorium would take on patients deemed criminally insane, who had made relatively small misdemeanors and had served their time, but on opening in 1885, the emphasis was on gentle therapy, daily routine and the upkeep of mid-Victorian structures of class and gender. Gentlemen could continue to assert their masculinity – thereby avoiding the demoralising sexless category of the invalid – by doing laps in the swimming pool, taking part in Swedish drill, or indulging in sociable games of billiards, golf, football, or cricket. Ladies, too, were encouraged to take gentle exercise, including archery and croquet. For the more creatively inclined, there were classes in oil painting, watercolours, photography and needlepoint, and exhibitions to proudly display the results. Creative expression remains an important part of occupational therapy.

Visits from brass bands, choirs and theatre groups made for a packed social calendar. The superintendant's journals read like a holiday camp: fetes, picnics, dances, dinner parties, and for those healthy enough, shopping trips and river excursions. Beachside properties were rented for the use of voluntary patients during the summer months for the benefits of fresh coastal air. Dr Rees Phillips was keen on purchasing a London property for putting up patients on overnight theatre trips, but this was never seriously considered by the board. This didn't stop the wealthier patients managing their own social lives; free to come and go, they eventually required an expansion of the sanatorium's stables for the private coaches taking these patients to and fro. The option of having close family members as boarding guests was encouraged. This was a modern facility, far from the nightmares of the past.

Life at Holloway Sanatorium was better than most of the patients knew on the outside. There were, of course, abuses of the '3-mile rule', including one gentleman being discovered several days after disappearing, wandering aimlessly around Derby racecourse. The Commissioners in Lunacy duly rapped the staff on the knuckles, and more care was taken in future, though it was not unknown for patients to take unwarranted sabbaticals to the local public houses, making a nuisance of themselves and no doubt having a marvellous time with their reputation as the local madmen.

However, it is important to note that Holloway Sanatorium was not revolutionary in this approach to activity. During the early 1880s, when Holloway Sanatorium first opened, the nearby Brookwood asylum for paupers laid on an extensive programme of readings, theatricals and social engagements, including marionette and conjuring shows. The monotony of the asylum was understood to be a hindrance to recovery, and entertainment was seen as an important part of rehabilitation. The Commissioners in Lunacy were disappointed to find patients less than thrilled by the possibility of mandatory exercise programmes, so dances and outdoor events were a pleasant method of tricking people into gentle physical therapy. Plus, as attendants were usually young, single and living on the premises entertainments helped to ease stress. Ditto, the beer allowance.

Of course, such a packed calendar of seemingly frivolous diversions made for a surreal spectacle, to visitors and new admissions alike: hundreds of men and women in varying states of mental distress watching puppet shows and whizzing around on ice skates. Patient records at Holloway give glimpses into the ups and downs of day-to-day life, how therapy was a joy to some and bewildering to others.

A dapper young man named Arthur Wilbraham Tollemache ('very eccentric in his manners and conversation') was initially encouraged to take up the violin as a practical means of dispelling his delusions of musical stardom. Tollemache's case notes dryly state his enthusiastic participation was 'extremely painful to anyone within earshot' and did nothing to quell his violent tendencies.

On a more tragic note, 22-year-old Agnes Alice Simmons was admitted to Holloway in 1890 with severe depression. Simmons wrote to her mother: 'When are you coming to take me home, I do not understand what this place is supposed to be & what I ought

26. Patient Alice Simmons on arrival in 1890.
(Wellcome Library, London)

to do, if you would come and take me home I would try to act sensible if it were possible & not worry you.' Alice turned to the library for comfort, but could only bring herself to read the same book over and over.

For all the good intentions behind Holloway Sanatorium, treatment of mental illness was still limited by ignorance, largely restricted to maintaining simple principals of comfort and safety. In all things, the importance of appropriate behaviour and manners were emphasised at Holloway. Normality had to be maintained as far as possible for patients to function comfortably on their release. The bedrooms were therefore designed to be homely, yet luxurious, to help patients see themselves as members of society and not lunatics living on the fringe. Occupation was vital, and in a middle-class context that meant simulating the kinds of polite conversations and social situations someone with a decent income could hope to enjoy in the outside world. To this end, the sanatorium employed about nine non-medical attendants at a time – male and female – whose job it was to make sure patients were dressed appropriately, and encouraged to converse, eat and generally live as normally as possible. In the Minutes of the House Committee, 3 January 1887, one such companion, Mister Mayne, was deemed to be unsuitable for his job following a bout of intemperance.

As for more interventional forms of treatment, developments in technology meant patients could expect electrical stimulation and chemical cures, including bromide, cannabis, and morphine injections, as well as more relaxing courses of massage and shower baths. There were more amenities at Holloway than the nearby public asylum, Brookwood, but this did not necessarily make for a better standard of care. The holiday atmosphere occasionally belied the seriousness of some patients' needs, and the staff – unused to dealing with middle-class, largely voluntary patients – were unsure of appropriate boundaries. This resulted in several successful suicides, or 'accidents', as they were recorded. Pauper asylums were generally better prepared for suicides in practical terms, insofar as there was less privacy, and staff were actively looking out for warning signs. There were padded rooms at Holloway, but no amount of restraint could substitute due diligence. The aforementioned Miss Simmons' records bear a warning of strong suicidal tendency. One elderly woman hanged herself with a rope left out by careless gardeners.

As an institution that relied on paying patients, Holloway Sanatorium was not exempt from dubious practices devised to protect reputation, particularly in the early days. Patients in states of high agitation were discouraged from writing home. Letters were intercepted before reaching the postman, and some containing complaints were never sent. In 1886, a 22-year-old man was forced to sneak letters past the staff:

> The worst has happened. I am in a lunatic asylum but I am perfectly sane only miserable … Oh the horror of this place. Can you picture me shut up here? Very shady practices go on in this place, and there are a number of people who have nothing the matter with them, except they have peculiar religious ideas, & their friends shut them up to get rid of them. I have been subject to awful indignities. I have to sleep in a room with about nine other fellows. I have to bath before a host of fellows, and if I am not civil I am locked up in close confinement. Oh the anguish I have suffered. My letters are tampered with & held back & I can get no redress … I implore you my only friend to pray for me in that I may be released from this awful prison.

The words 'awful' and 'prison' were certainly not good for business, particularly when the founder was known for his quack medicine. Life as an involuntary patient was clearly unpleasant, particularly when – as in this man's case – the reason for admission was a family argument. If a family were willing to pay to temporarily offload a troublesome party, the sanatorium staff were not above playing along.

By 1890, there were 292 patients and boarders recorded at Holloway. Of the 193 new patients admitted during that year, a third suffered from anxiety or depression, and another third exhibited some form of 'hereditary insanity', which could include anything from autism to congenital syphilis. A small percentage of the patients were alcoholic and a handful had brain injuries or sunstroke. By 1890, the law required the sanatorium to record instances of mechanical restraint, so we know three new patients were wrapped in wet linen, two were straitjacketed, and seven had their hands restrained with sets of specially designed locked gloves to prevent self-harm or masturbation. The solitary vice was still considered a cause of mental illness well into the twentieth century, and these latter unfortunates spent a total of 169 hours 'gloved'. In that year also, nine patients died at Holloway – this was the lowest number of deaths recorded at the sanatorium.

Intriguingly, Crossland's plans for the sanatorium neglected to include a chapel – something that was required by law. Thomas harboured ill feeling towards the clergy all his life, for reasons unclear. Perhaps it was a simple oversight. Or perhaps Thomas and George Martin had taken note of the 'religious mania' especially prevalent amongst women admitted to asylums. One such patient at Holloway – Olivia Caroline Robertson – was admitted in 1889, exhibiting a marked tremor. The photograph in her case notes shows her turned away from the camera, hands clasped in prayer. Religious mania could be exacerbated by the presence of clergy, who, finding themselves among the suffering, all too often gave sermons that – according to Dr Joseph Mortimer Granville, who patented an electromechanical vibrator for the treatment of hysteria – were 'so prosy, so ill-judged, and above all so monotonous, that it must take a week of pleasant intercourse with patients to wipe it out completely.' Before the sanatorium's opening, The Commissioners in Lunacy (probably the highly Evangelical Earl of Shaftesbury himself) duly ordered Thomas to have a chapel tacked on to the side of the building, and the project was treated with the same aesthetic vision as the rest of the sanatorium. Christian patients could continue to worship almost as they would have before admittance, though death was a subject strictly out of bounds for asylum pulpits. Life was encouraged to continue.

Thomas would never see the sanatorium's grand opening in 1885. He died an old man in 1883, and so we can only imagine how he would have steered the institution's management. What he left was an asylum in the truest sense of the word – somewhere optimistic, forward-looking, at least *trying* to be more compassionate than those that had come before. However, the project wasn't all selfless philanthropy. The sanatorium was built deliberately close to the railway lines, along with an eye-catching billboard for Holloway's chief concern: pills and ointment. Public interest in the project had been building throughout the 1870s, with the extravagant façade doing its own publicity by simply existing. Illustrations

THE LATE MR. THOMAS HOLLOWAY.

27. Thomas in his seventies, taken from *The Illustrated London News*.
(Verity Holloway)

of the building circulated to newspapers came complete with a portrait of Thomas himself, looking every inch the stern Victorian patriarch. None too flattering, said a few recipients, but the effect was deliberate – Thomas Holloway was now more than simply a tenacious businessman. He had re-invented himself as part of the establishment. His was a legacy that would outlast the posters choking the nation's walls.

The staff of *Punch*, naturally, were tickled. Only the dangerously insane would trust 'Professor' Holloway to cure them in his ill-gotten palace. They generously suggested an inscription for above the door:

> *Not oft is fate so just – see wealth restored*
> *Back to the simple source from which it poured!*

But the jokes were drowned out by praise coming in from all over the nation. It was hard to write the sanatorium off as the vanity project of a quack when it had the support of the Prime Minister. When it was reported that Holloway had spent £300,000 of his personal fortune – barely putting a dent in it – the papers had to marvel. Never had a quack taken such a direction before. Holloway Sanatorium would continue to admit patients until 1980, a hundred years after its inception.

Jane Holloway laid the sanatorium's foundation stone. A ward was named after her, with a matching one named for Thomas. The Holloways' marriage had entered its third decade, and Thomas was as impressed by his 'Grace Darling' as when they'd first met. Jane's willingness to work towards his dreams – not to mention her tolerance for his strenuous work schedule – made her the ideal Victorian wife. Her common sense and modesty were qualities that kept the pair of them with their feet on the ground even when their fortune was beyond anything either had dreamt of, and her good humour kept Thomas from falling too deeply into the melancholic spells he was prone to. Both were now entering old age, having come from humble beginnings into wealth and fame. Yet despite their good fortune, they lived plainly, and were happiest that way. The sanatorium was to be their monument – an impressive one by anyone's standards. But even before the sanatorium was officially opened, Thomas had embarked upon another project; one even more ambitious as the first, and which paid tribute to the steadfast women in his life.

Chapter 10

The Handsomest College in England

I do not want art for a few; any more than education for a few; or freedom for a few.

William Morris, 1877

As doctor and Harvard professor Edward Clarke wrote in his 1873 book *Sex in Education*, it was a fact that 'a woman's body could only handle a limited number of developmental tasks at one time – that girls who spent too much energy developing their minds during puberty would end up with undeveloped or diseased reproductive systems.'

It may, therefore, have been a surprise to many readers, in the winter of 1874, to find papers all over Britain running the following announcement:

> I am informed that in addition to the new sanatorium for the insane which Mr Holloway of world wide pill notoriety is busy erecting at a cost of something like £100,000 at St Anne's Heath, Virginia Water, he contemplates building a new University for ladies on an estate at Egham, which he has purchased for £25,000, and that he has charged an architect to draw up the necessary plans. It is understood the whole affair will cost £150,000. The plans are far advanced, and the foundations will shortly be commenced. The new University is intended for high-class education for ladies, and will be administered on the University plan, and the founder intends it to be in every way 'the handsomest college in England'.

Perhaps 'notorious' wasn't Thomas's choice of epithet. Some went with the more flattering 'great pill merchant', but the note of incredulity remained. The founding of a women's college was a radical act. When Thomas embarked upon the creation of a women's university, the education of girls and women was a highly controversial subject, in social and medical circles. Consider the first full degrees were only awarded to British women in the 1940s. Even then, the bluestocking straw woman still loomed large in the public consciousness as a figure of fun, an old maid reaching beyond her grasp. In the mid-nineteenth century, a woman who hankered after an education was a creature deserving of no less than revulsion, as this opinion piece from the *Quarterly Review* demonstrates:

> It is the ostentation of knowledge, and not the knowledge itself, which disgusts, and is doubly offensive when female aspirants are voluble on subjects of which they understand little – except perhaps the jargon. Pretention is repulsive where we look for reserve, and the woman purchases knowledge too dearly who exchanges it for the attributes which are the charm of her sex.

The prevailing Victorian belief in the physical and mental delicacy of females was cited as a reason to bar women from higher education, and even simple exercise. A woman's brain was thought to be 150 grams lighter than a man's, and the womb at risk from literal destruction as a result of an overtaxed mind. However, there were plenty who challenged those myths. Women's periodicals would frequently remind their readers that gentle exercise was perfectly acceptable during menstruation and otherwise recommended for strength and overall health. Familiarly, the lived experience of womanhood contradicted male conservative opinion. Elizabeth Garrett Anderson, who had become England's first qualified female physician and surgeon in the mid-1860s, wrote a stinging riposte to Edward Clark's *Sex in Education*. If a woman's womb could atrophy so easily, how was it that lower-class manual workers faired well enough on their periods, with no more fertility problems than anyone else? All this talk of delicacy was class-based superstition. It was *boredom* that posed a significant risk to the health of young women, she argued. Confined to the home, with few prospects and diversions, girls had been proven to deteriorate in body and mind, turning to self-harm to act out their frustrations. Women wanted to learn. No amount of male hectoring would change that.

But men were not the only obstacles to women's education. Novelist and social commentator Margaret Oliphant believed in votes for women. However, she held contrary views on the conduct of young ladies hoping to use learning as a ladder:

> Equality is the mightiest of humbugs – there is no such thing in existence; and the idea of opening up the professions and occupations and governments of men to women, seems to us the vainest as well as the vulgarest of chimeras. God has ordained visibly, by all the arrangements in nature and providence, one sphere and kind of work for a man and another for a woman.

Ever since Mary Wollstonecraft penned *Vindication of the Rights of Women*, there were women like Oliphant ready to stand up and contradict her. What would happen to the fabric of society if the 'shrieking sisterhood' had their way, carrying on like men? Who would raise healthy children and support hardworking husbands? A vital part of the role of womanhood in society was self-effacement; this was to be respected, not mourned. If a girl dreamt of a man's education and worldly esteem, she simply wasn't adept at reigning in her passions. Sensation novels with feisty heroines were all very well as far-fetched entertainment, but if every governess who dreamt of wearing Jane Eyre's shoes got her way, what would happen to society? And even if she could go to university and earn a degree, would she be happy? As Harriett Martineau wrote in 1855, Wollstonecraft was 'a poor victim of passion, with no control over her own peace, and no calmness or content except when the needs of her individual nature were satisfied.'

It was easy to score points against ambitious young women. Critics believed the desire for an education merely proved their failings in other, far more important areas, such as beauty and charm. In the decades leading up to Thomas Holloway's decision to build a women's university, the education of women had been limited to their eventual role in the home, or, for girls from less well-off families, the skills required for the work of a governess; another home-based role. *Being* was more important than *knowing*. Sarah Ellis, another vehement anti-feminist of the Victorian age, took this to an extreme that reads like a manifesto of self-loathing. A woman's whole life was 'one of feeling, rather than of action; whose highest duty is so often to suffer, and be still; whose deepest enjoyments are all relative; who has nothing, and is nothing of herself; whose experience, if unparticipated, is a total blank.'

Holloway College was not the first of its kind in Britain. In Hertfordshire, Hitchin College – later to become Cambridge's Girton College – was established with just nine students in 1869. The founders – Emily Davies, a suffragist and campaigner for women's education, Barbara Bodichon, artist and friend of the Pre-Raphaelite circle, and Lady Henrietta Stanley, political salon hostess – wished to prove that women could pass the entrance exams of Oxford or Cambridge. This pioneering move surprisingly met with little resistance, as a pass at one of these exams did not imply the admission of female students to either institution. Before the establishment of Hitchin, female students could take a general 'Pass degree', constituting a mish-mash of a variety of subjects, or a more challenging Honours degree focusing on mathematics, natural sciences, or classics. Neither counted as a 'real' degree. Emily Davies felt this concession to women's higher education wasn't enough, and that, given the chance, a female student could pass the Tripos examination qualifying them for further study towards a Bachelor's degree. With the help of a wealthy Trinity College alumnus, ninety-one female students were permitted to take the Cambridge Local Examination in 1865, and in 1873, three students of Hitchin unofficially took and passed the Tripos. Despite proving themselves in the exam hall, Rachel Cook, Louisa Lumsden and Sarah Woodhead do not appear on official Cambridge class lists, but their memory is still celebrated in a song after the College Feast:

> *Whenever we go forward*
> *A hard exam to try*
> *Their memory goes before us*
> *To raise our courage high*
> *They made old Cambridge wonder;*
> *Then let us give three cheers*
> *For Woodhead, Cook, and Lumsden*
> *The Girton Pioneers*

Nevertheless, Hitchin College remained situated outside of Cambridge so not to cause controversy with its mere presence. Anna Lloyd, one of the first Hitchin students, recalled a priest in a railway carriage pointing out the college as 'That infidel place!'

When women's higher education encroached upon the Cambridge bubble, male students lynched an effigy of a woman in her underwear from a window of what is now the University Bookshop. The dummy was riding a typical student bicycle. A mock funeral was held, complete with a draped coffin – symbolising, presumably, the death of homosocial education – and paraded through the streets. Even as late as the 1940s, when Hitchin became Girton and was received into the canon of Cambridge colleges, female students had to juggle their studies with harassment; derision focused on their looks, their suitability as wives and mothers, and accusations of lesbian activity. In the 1870s, when Thomas Holloway became interested in the issue, the dominant narrative was that normal women wanted babies and the domestic sphere. A woman who wished to learn was suspect, laughable, but most of all, faulty.

So why was a purveyor of quack medicine like Thomas Holloway hoping to spend hundreds of thousands of pounds on a college for women? According to legend, Jane is to thank for her husband taking this unexpected direction. Despite the vast sum spent on the sanatorium, there was so much left of the Holloway riches that the two of them could never have spent it in their old age, even if they had decided to live in complete opulence. When Thomas wondered aloud which needy sector of society could benefit from his fortune, Jane is said to have told her husband that women 'are the greatest sufferers.' This statement sadly isn't elaborated on, but it was nonetheless true that like invalids and the mad, women were treated as second-class citizens, languishing in a category of their own with little hope of advancement beyond marriage. Even then, before the Married Woman's Property Act of 1870, a woman's savings, earnings, and property went automatically to her husband, a legal humiliation redolent of Sarah Ellis's vision of womanhood: a non-person 'who has nothing, and is nothing.'

If Thomas really wished to do social good with his money, something for the benefit of women would be ideal. He already had a model in mind to emulate. Across the Atlantic, a vast and beautiful college had been built on the instruction of self-made millionaire Mathew Vassar. Like Thomas, he made his money in a sector entirely unrelated to education (in his case, beer) and had no heir. 'I wish somebody would tell me what to do with my money,' Vassar complained. 'It's the plague of my life.' On a trip to London in the 1840s, Vassar beheld Guy's Hospital in Southwark and was deeply touched by the plaque commemorating the benevolent founder. Whether it was the Christian message or the ego intoxicant of having one's name held up as a paragon of goodness, Vassar returned to America eager to spend his fortune. Coincidentally, he too originally planned to build a hospital, but a female friend awakened him to 'the possibility and necessity' of a seat of higher learning exclusively for women. There had always been a streak in Thomas's personality that would see someone else's good idea and want to do it a hundred times better. Vassar, it seemed to him, was his American counterpart and new rival.

Jane's role in Holloway College has since been downplayed. Very little of her correspondence still exists, so we make do with a vague outline of a woman who seems to have been kind and genial, who sent gift baskets to the local poor, and enjoyed singing after family dinners. Most likely, she was not a vocal radical when it came to the rights of her sex. Jane had no special education to speak of and we cannot guess her reading habits. But when taken next to the mainstream statements of Oliphant, Ellis, and their ilk, persuading one's wealthy husband to donate an immense sum towards the education of women – and to put his name on it – must be interpreted as a radical act. All the more so when Thomas's exact plans were outlined.

Thomas acquired a print copy of one of Vassar's speeches, in which he said:

> It occurred to me that woman, having received from her Creator the same intellectual constitution as man has the same right to intellectual culture and development. I considered that the mothers of this country mould the character of its citizens, determine its institutions, and shape its destiny.

Thomas was thinking big, as usual. The Ladies' University, as he called it in the beginning, was to be to women's education what Oxford and Cambridge were to men's. As for training women for lonely lives as governesses – absolutely not. These were real degrees for real scholars with real ambitions.

Two years after committing to the project, Thomas wrote to his acquaintance David Chadwick, MP for Macclesfield:

> Most of us who do well, are indebted in early youth to the teaching of our mothers – and how much better it might be to the human family if mothers of the next generation should possess a high-class education – and if anyone took a degree would not her boys and

girls be formed of such a habit? and say: Mother whatever you have done in the way of learning, we will strive to emulate you.

Perhaps Thomas was thinking of his experiments in his mother's Cornish kitchen as he wrote. Maybe she encouraged him to make a business out of his early trials with grease and pungent herbs. Vassar, like Holloway, appreciated that wives and mothers had great influence in the home, and that a good education would ensure fewer young Americans would grow up to be illiterate and possibly criminal. The role of motherhood was not something Thomas wished education to replace, but nonetheless, his logic is sound. A generation of more intellectual, ambitious boys and girls would no doubt do wonderful things for the nation as a whole. It wasn't exactly a feminist utopia that the two men had in mind, but it is worth noting how both were inspired by women close to them at roughly the same time.

While it's debatable that Thomas Holloway was a radical in terms of gender equality, he certainly associated with radical reformers. James Beal, a man instrumental in government reforms during the 1870s, acted as PR agent for both the sanatorium and the college. Known as something of a live wire, and not above stretching the truth to strengthen his political attacks on the bored and corrupt denizens of Westminster, Beal appreciated how the class system hindered intelligent working-class men from reaching their potential. Lecturing at various working men's clubs in Chelsea, he remarked how the debates that went on there – anything from Shakespeare to science – practically made these evening clubs a working men's university. It was no coincidence that these clubs were closely tied to trade unions. These were men with a fire for improvement. For the male working classes and the female sex alike, disenfranchisement could lead to ambition. There was never any concern that the proposed Holloway College would lack students.

Thomas was the first to admit he had no clue as to how a college ought to be run. But he was eager to learn the best possible scheme.

On 10 February 1875, James Beal invited a number of politicians and educators to Holloway's New Oxford Street office. This meeting included a number of prominent women activists, some of whom would go on to be well-known Suffragettes: Millicent Fawcett, Maria Grey, Dr Elizabeth Garrett Anderson and Emily Davies (not to be mistaken for Emily Davison, who would later be trampled by a horse at the Epsom Derby). Suffragettes would later ironically refer to prison time in the coincidentally named Holloway Prison as 'getting one's Holloway degree'. Two MPs also attended, one of whom – Chadwick – brought along William Hague, one of Vassar's charter trustees. Hague had legendarily received from Vassar the enormous sum for building his college in a humble tin box. James Beal used his own knowledge and contacts to help pick the guests, prompting Thomas to ask him, concerning Maria Grey, 'Would you have the goodness to tell me who and what she is?'

It was a controversial selection of guests, and the evening's discussion led to a firm decision that the college should be founded on 'studies and sciences which the experience of modern times has shown to be the most valuable' – mathematics, history, Latin, French, German, and English composition to name a few. All teaching staff would be female, including the principal, who had absolute power. It was hoped that, although Oxford University did not confer degrees on women until the 1920s, about half the student body of Holloway College would go on to take exams at Oxford. Otherwise, there was London University, which did recognise women and would eventually merge with Holloway in 1900. The women present at that meeting – Garrett Anderson, Grey, Davies and Fawcett – had already tried and failed to convince Parliament and the press of women's rights to higher education and the vote. To have their ideas so readily made manifest must have been exhilarating. Maria Grey deplored the idea of a woman gaining an education to attract a better class of husband, and Emily Davies had herself already published on the importance of granting equal qualifications to men and women. This, to the best of their ability, was the aim of

28. Elizabeth Garrett Anderson, caricatured in 'Medical Women's Federation', *The Graphic*, 1872, looking every inch the stern bluestocking.
(Wellcome Library, London)

Holloway College, and Thomas was more than happy to put his name on such a venture.

Crossland was the obvious choice for the project's architect. By then, he was on 'my boy' terms with Thomas, but the best was always expected, and on the few occasions Crossland erred, Thomas was quicker to give a ticking off than before. This may have had something to do with Crossland's personal life. It was around this time that the architect found himself an extramarital diversion in the form of Londoner Eliza Ruth Hatt. Eighteen years Crossland's junior, Hatt had married at the age of sixteen to a colleague of her father's, and her affair with Crossland was no passing fling. She bore him a total of three sons, the first of which she openly named after Crossland, husband be damned. When Crossland's wife died in 1879, he ensconced himself and his mistress at the college permanently, in a comparatively grotty little bungalow that was demolished in 2015 to make way for a new library. Hatt would ultimately be memorialised alongside Crossland's wife at Highgate Cemetery, as 'wife, companion, friend', despite no evidence the pair ever made their relationship legally binding. Eliza Ruth Hatt was known as an actress, though there is no evidence she ever trod the boards. Perhaps she was referred to as such by the other women at the college – actresses were said to have loose morals.

Crossland was present at the meeting with the educated women. Despite his own unconventional living arrangements, he evidently found the activists rather tiresome, and later complained that the only thing that tempered Holloway's zeal for doing exactly what they said was a low fever that left him temporarily bedridden. The ladies laid out very particular plans for architecture and ornamentation, but Crossland managed to veto many of them during his employer's fever. While Holloway Sanatorium was Flemish Gothic in appearance, Crossland had his eye on a more French look for the college:

> Now it appeared to me that a return either to the purer classical styles or to the Renaissance of the 16th century was certainly

impending. When, therefore, Mr Holloway invited me to submit to him illustrations of such ancient buildings as I thought suitable in style and character for the proposed College I selected views of chateaux in the valley of the Loire, as well as that of Fontainebleau; and these I submitted, placing Chambord first. The effect on Mr Holloway was somewhat startling. After some complimentary remarks as to my judgment, he told me that he was advised to put the design to competition, but would like to hear from me the course I should take in the event of my becoming a competitor. I replied that I should visit the Touraine, and, with an assistant, sketch and measure Chambord in the completest way: also such portions of other chateaux as appeared to me useful in the study of the style and containing characteristics not found at Chambord. He then said, 'Will you do this Mr Crossland?' To which I answered most assuredly I would. He then patted me on the shoulder, and said, 'My boy, you shall have the work; but mind, on the condition that you sketch and measure Chambord from bottom to top. No more competitions for me. I had too much trouble about the last. When will you start?' My reply was that as soon as I could set matters quite straight at the Sanatorium I would start. In this way came to me the most important work of my life; and I shortly afterwards left with my principal assistant, Mr Taylor, for the scene of action, Mr Holloway having stated his intention to join us at Chambord on hearing from us that our work was completed.

But that work was of much too pleasant a character to be hurried, and some six weeks elapsed before I reported it finished. Shortly afterwards we met Mr Holloway, then over eighty years of age, at Blois, he having travelled through Paris direct ... Mr Holloway having spent two days in going round and through the building checking off our sketch-books, feature by feature, and finding only one bit of work missing, viz, a small dormer window on the east front which we could not get at easily – but which had to be got at before our work could be passed – we started on a tour of inspection to Cheverny, Blois again, Amboise, Chaumont, Chenonceaux, Valencay, Versailles, Fontainebleau, and, having made large purchases of photographs and books in Paris, we made for home.

29. Photograph of Holloway College as it appeared not long after opening.
(Verity Holloway)

Even in his late seventies, Thomas was an energetic traveller and a stickler for detail. And detail was something the college certainly would not lack. Since described as 'flamboyant beyond belief' and 'the Taj Mahal of Egham', the completed building is a red bricked hybrid of cathedral turrets, opulent Georgian terraces, the conical roofs of a French chateau, and ornamentation that wouldn't be out of place in a royal palace or an especially feverish playboy's mansion. In Thomas's own words, this was a building to 'beat Vassar into fits' and make the Rothschild mansion look puny by comparison. Dragons and winged lions line the rooftops, along with cherubs, serpents, stern rams and stone crocodiles apparently carved by someone who had never seen one. There was barely a square foot without a flourish or scroll, but there was method to this flamboyance: the Founder's Building is arranged in a double quadrant emulating Trinity College at Cambridge, and has a similar symmetry of decoration. Inside the quadrangle, each corner features a different patriarch – Pope Julius II, Mohammad, Confucius and

Savonarola – and each is assigned his own element, earth, air, fire, or water. The water tower, containing a large cistern, is embellished appropriately with aquatic life; storks and entwined fish alongside the unavoidable quatrefoils and flourishes. Symmetrical cloisters and wide balustrades give sweeping views of the quadrangle's interior and impressive skyline, as well as the rich symbolism affirming the building's noble purpose. Above the main doors are images of poetry and science, commerce and medicine. In the lower quadrant, the eastern pediment pays tribute to Surrey's agricultural renown along with a bust of Holloway himself, based on one of Napoleon in the Louvre. (Read into that what you wish.) Beneath a classical depiction of charity and education is the self-appointed Holloway family motto, *Nil Desperandum.* Never despair. Surrey would be famous for his endeavours, now.

For a seat of higher education – especially one for women, barred from Oxbridge by their sex – Crossland's symbolically rich, if slightly manic design was ideal. *The Builder,* however, had fewer kind words than Thomas and Crossland would have liked:

> Much of the ornament ... is coarse and heavy, and the proportions of many of the windows and openings are much lower than we are accustomed to consider correct. The omission of the bed-mould of the main cornice, leaving merely a row of exaggerated details, though there is some precedent for it, is not a successful device, and the capping of the small circular angle-buttresses of the main central pavilions is absolutely ugly.

Neo-Gothic, for all its modern reputation as a cornerstone of the Victorian age, was not universally adored. Inside, however, the décor was surprisingly muted, and the living quarters were appointed for comfort and for sociability, with plenty of space for hosting tea parties. Elizabeth Garrett Anderson herself stipulated that all students should have a sitting room of their own for healthy breaks between studying. There were a total of 760 fireplaces, with 700 chimneys, and teachers lived amongst their students in an effort to foster friendliness and banish any illusion of the college as a boarding school – these were young ladies, not schoolgirls. Certain elements of boarding school discipline remained, however: students were expected to attend gym twice a week, and have their weight and measurements recorded every term. This was ostensibly to be sure no student's health was damaged by 'strong brain work', but one suspects such records were useful in dispelling the myth of the deteriorating bluestocking body.

Former students from the early days of Holloway College remembered the sense of sisterhood amongst the students with fondness. Class snobbery was roundly condemned, and the influence of families at home – some of whom were not wholly supportive of their daughters' academic direction – was kept to a minimum. The college, Emily Davies said, was a taste of freedom, setting students up for a future of self-reliance and social responsibility. Holloway College would offer students freedom to study, freedom to socialise, and the freedom to blossom into bright, happy young women. 'I will try to be respectful of parents,' Davies wrote, 'but how is it possible to describe College life without showing how infinitely pleasanter it will be than home?'

The papers, naturally, continued their tirades against 'English Old Maids', which included anyone twenty-five and unmarried, particularly those with academic pretentions:

> These troublesome females embrace the thankless career of the bluestocking because they have never found anything better to embrace … An old maid is a social fiasco, and in England almost a social blister. She blocks the public way when she proceeds to set herself up as an institution – a system – and claims the right to put her hand to the helm.

Steering her own vessel, the bluestocking put herself in society's centre rather than demurely fading away at the right hand of a husband. The girls at Holloway College gave little credence to the papers. They were delighted to be setting themselves up in their comfortable, convivial lodgings amongst like-minded souls. Early photographs show the rooms crammed with home comforts and knickknacks, some of which would make chauvinist journalists' heads spin. Swords and masculine hunting trophies hung on the walls, along with the occasional tasteful male nude. 'Families' of girls formed, like clubs, as Kathleen Vinall, a 1920s student, recalled:

> There was the most strict taboo of not being friends out of your year. A taboo that I broke! I happened to meet somebody on my first or second day who spoke to me and said, 'Would you like to join our family?', and I found myself in a group ... lived over on East ... who just by a little chance happened to come together. Families were chiefly for tea. And they felt loyalty towards each other.

Love affairs naturally bloomed between the students, some of which were only half-heartedly clandestine. A maths student recorded her affairs in her diary:

> 19 June 1906. Baby came and sat on my knee ... but I will draw a veil over the rest of the evening ...
> 23 June 1906. We tried to find a secluded spot, so after a bit we got into a sort of wood and lay down under a huge tree, with my umbrella over us, and I am ashamed to say, flirted terribly.

Such relationships initially went unnoticed as platonic 'sentimental devotions' between girls, but as the twentieth century rolled on, suspicions of the staff increased. The diarist and another girl were almost caught in one another's arms by a teacher. Having a 'pash' was one thing, but the prevailing belief held that young women first had to be aware of sexual immorality to go on to commit it, and the well-read were at high risk of discovering Sapphic romance. Unlike male homosexuality, lesbianism was not a crime in Britain at the end of the nineteenth century, but expressions of romantic love between girl students could lead to expulsion; or rather, being sent home 'for care', sometimes psychiatric, like an unnamed student at Westfield College in 1883. As late as 1926, the academic and author Marie Carmichael Stopes warned female students against indulging their desires for fellow academics. Turn, if you must, to 'self abuse', she wrote. Anything but the cult of homosexuality. Visions of Holloway Sanatorium and locked gloves come to mind.

As with the sanatorium, there was initially no plan to employ a pastor at the college. The question of religion is an intriguing facet of Thomas's character. Like Vassar, who built a number of churches, he did not attend church if he could help it. During the whole of 1877, a friend noted, he did not attend a single service. Neither was he an atheist. On the contrary: he claimed to have 'witnessed the hand of God in all things.' So what was he trying to do by creating a church-less college after a church-less hospital? One possibility lies in a letter stating he wanted no one denomination to take precedent over another. Such a thing could create factions within the student body, requiring students to make a show of their devotion to please parents or peers, causing their work to suffer. Another is that religious conservatives were known to actively discourage women from studying with the 'separate but equal' argument, citing the obedience of Jesus's mother and the restrictive teachings of Saint Paul. 'Separate but equal' was the idea that home and motherhood were not necessarily lesser spheres than academia, but simply more true to nature, and to be celebrated in their own right. As a deterrent it was more powerful than plain mockery, as it reinforced the social conditioning instilled in girls from birth, particularly the desire to serve and to take pleasure in quiet usefulness. An article in *The Christian Remembrancer* in 1864 concludes that because both mortal men and God were above women, knowing this, a woman had the 'pleasure in submission, in bowing to authority, in the consciousness that her trust outstrips her reason'. A real college with real degrees couldn't be more at odds with this, and a resident clergyman may well have worked to discourage the female students in small, gradually erosive ways.

Even if Thomas personally vetted a radical pastor, there was no guarantee his successor would carry on in the same vein after Thomas's death. Eventually bowing to criticism, Thomas agreed to employ a clergyman who would preach a general spectrum of Christianity, 'offensive to no one', in the gilded Byzantine chapel with its dramatic chequered floor.

As Thomas watched his two great public works take shape before him, he reflected on his own rise to prominence. The London staff of Holloway, in their palatial workplace with all the perks of a generous employer, later recalled the day Professor Holloway regaled them with his origin story. The old man wanted to encourage them in their work towards the company's continuing success, but also to take pride in themselves as individuals. 'My object in communicating to them my early beginnings is merely for their edification as showing what small beginnings may lead to, by ability, perseverance, and industry,' he explained. The assembled porters, clerks, shop girls, and forewomen were then presented with handfuls of shiny shillings. Without too much sentimentality, Thomas regarded his employees as a father might, and wanted them to take the unlikely story of his success as their own. As Thomas had already said, he had seen the hand of God at work in all things. But what God gives, he may also take away.

Chapter 11

Bold Beggars

And so, Thomas Holloway, who had grown up mopping spillages in his parents' pub, found himself being hailed as the greatest humanitarian the world had ever known. 'Generous, noble-hearted philanthropist!' the papers called him. This overexcitement spread from continent to continent. In Buenos Aires, he was hailed as a great and good man worthy of immortality alongside the gods of wisdom and medicine. Closer to home, in Stockport, Shakespeare was invoked:

> It has been said that some men are born great, some achieve greatness, and others have greatness thrust upon them. A more remarkable of the second of these classes, I think, it would be difficult to find in that of Thomas Holloway, whose pills and ointment are household words in every civilised age, and every uncivilised country in the world. In the Wilds of Tartary, the Siberian Desert, the Celestial Empire, yea in the very mountains of the moon, are the praises of the great pilular deity Holloway sung, and his name blessed in every known and unknown tongue as the 'mighty healer'.

Can we detect a grain of irony? Surely most people knew the pilular deity's cures were as dubious as his divinity. What really caused the stir was Holloway's unconventional method of disposing of his money. It was a moral turnaround of Dickensian proportions. Whatever his enemies wished to say about his medicines, they could hardly fault Holloway's philanthropy. The household name was now – arguably, at least – respectable.

The 1870s were a most prosperous decade for the Holloway family. Had Thomas and Jane been the socialising sort, they would now have found themselves mixing with the upper echelons of Victorian middle-class society. Instead, the pair took the occasional trip to the Thames, called in on Jane's sister Mary Ann, and took quiet drives in their carriage. When Thomas saw what the papers had to say about his wealth, he was mildly annoyed by the vulgarity of it all, especially the speculations about what kind of wild private life he must be leading with all that spare cash. Thomas liked billiards and dogs, and preferred his wine watered down. But that didn't make for much of a story. The tall, softly-spoken Cornishman finally objected when *The Kentish Observer* fabricated a story about him having once been a butler, only because it was an important point of pride that he be known as a man who had always relied on his own initiative. Being a humble servant certainly would have added an extra layer of fascination to the Holloway story, but Thomas had never been one for sensationalism where his personal life was concerned.

A photograph taken of Thomas around this time displays his characteristic melancholy. Like the 1845 portrait by William Scott, his cheekbones protrude with a faint smile, but the hint of cockiness is long gone. He dispensed with the flashy tie pin and expensive tailoring, choosing instead a casual pose with riding crop in hand. The faraway look, once speaking of ambition and confidence, shows a man with too many cares. Before embarking on the college and sanatorium, Thomas had written to friends in France of his weariness of money talk:

> You say I have a gold mine. If so, it is but a very small one. Is a miner's life to be desired, always digging and plodding, and even if he does bring forth some lucre, is it really worth the cost and anxiety and time he takes to get it ... the gold I get I cannot eat or use about myself, so after all of what value is it to me. This I think is a real piece of philosophy.

Having spent about £600,000 on philanthropic projects, one would hope Thomas must have felt at least a little satisfaction to see his fortune put to use. Any other man would have retired, embarked on a Grand Tour, or at least used his remaining funds to settle down in comfort and enjoy the peaceful gardens of Tittenhurst Park. But this was the man who had once landed himself in gaol over a petty rivalry. Thomas was old now, and wiser by far, but a new figure had entered his life that awoke that innate dogged determination.

'Joseph Haydock is a great scoundrel, he has put me to an expense in one way or another of at least $100,000.'

Thus Thomas complained to the American press. One hundred thousand was no measly sum. Having already visited America and thoroughly explored opportunities for distribution there, Thomas decided that North America was the one place he had no interest in. The nation was already inundated with quacks going all-out in their attempts to beguile the public with the fads of the day. Indeed, the market there was so permissive that American quacks were frequently surprised to find the rest of the world so anti-quack by comparison. In America, corrupt clergymen were paid to praise nostrums from the pulpit. The problem was so widespread, eventually the archbishops attempted to intervene – to no avail. American quacks liked to employ vague Oriental imagery, hanging on the coat-tails of the popularity of Willow Pattern china towards the end of the nineteenth century. One such cure-all ointment, 'Sapanule', was promoted with illustrations of Japanese mothers doting on fat children, all wearing an approximation of traditional dress in a happy domestic setting amongst reeds and water fountains. 'So different from deluging the stomach with drugs,' one ad promises, echoing the alternative medicine promises of today, citing nameless 'chemicals' as being harmful whilst touting its own secret, almost magical recipe. It was all reminiscent of the showy exoticism Albinolo had been fond of, and by the time Thomas was rich enough to expand his business in the foreign market, he was already considering respectable investments like the sanatorium, where such showmanship would do him no favours. There was little to be gained in entering the American market, so Thomas elected an agent in New York – one Joseph Haydock – to manage exports for interested European travellers and immigrants, and leave it at that.

Unfortunately, this disinterest left a vacuum for fraudsters. Success breeds parasites, and while the sanatorium was still a pile of bricks, Haydock quietly severed ties with his employer and took the Holloway name into his own hands. Thomas was alerted to the fraud by browsing his collection of international newspapers, and immediately fired off a riposte:

> You will greatly oblige me & the American Public if you will be pleased to denounce [Haydock] in your paper as a knave & a cheat & that he is using my name to my detriment & for the purpose of passing off spurious imitations of my remedies of the Public. I have heard he pays no one.

It was already too late. 'The blue pill' was one of the most common American home remedies of the 1860s and 70s, recommended by their manufacturers for anything from giddiness to syphilis. Despite being advertised as a mainstay of the caricatured robust Native American, Tibetan monk, and wise Indian guru, blue pills were anything but a gentle natural remedy. They were, of course, mercury. Though immensely popular, there were enough cases of accidental poisoning and horrendous side effects to make room for opponents.

Rivals of blue pills offered an alternative in the form of 'herbal' drinks, which were largely sugar and strong alcohol. With the American public seemingly stuck between being poisoned and perennially drunk, it was natural that savvy advertisers would use these fears to push their own remedies, regardless of the ingredients. In 1856, an advert appeared in the American press attacking a well-known mercury quack:

Abernathy's insidious remedy, blue pill, invades the system with a mineral poison, while HOLLOWAY'S great medicine composed exclusively of vegetable extracts regulates every internal function, and leaves no sting behind.

A year earlier, a similar advert appears in the New Orleans Commercial Bulletin:

THE AMERICAN'S FRIEND!! Holloway's Pills. To the citizens of the United States: I most humbly and sincerely thank you for the immense patronage which you have bestowed upon my Pills. I take the opportunity of stating that my ancestors were all American citizens, and that I entertain for all concerns America and the Americans the most lively sympathies, so much so that I originally compounded these Pills expressly to suit your climate habits, constitutions and manner of living, intending to establish myself amongst you, which I have now done by taking premises in New York.

It was a bold fraud, not least for listing Thomas Holloway's actual Strand address before directing inquiries towards an unconnected American wholesaler in Manhattan. The claim that Holloway himself had American blood suggests Haydock may well have been hard at work impersonating his former employer in the flesh, as Henry Holloway once had. This wasn't Haydock's first foray into the world of quack medicine. He had previously set himself up as Doctor Haydock, creator of Haydock's New Liver Pills, with an international advertising campaign. A testimonial in the *New Zealand Observer* sounded remarkably familiar in its fulsome praise, if applied with all the finesse of a sledgehammer:

Honoured and Learned Physician:
The Unworthy one who dares to address you and come before you humbly in the dust, begs for his people (caste) that you would deign to look upon their ignoble miseries and cure them with your life-giving grains (Pills). Illustrious one, your most potent medicine

is life to them and their children, and all the Drug Bazaars are empty, and your soul is not in them. This humble petitioner, though he is ignoble and unworthy to be in your high presence, prays that you will gratuitously permit your life grains (Pills) to come to Aykab.

'Doctor' Haydock – the man who claimed his medical discovery equalled steam, telegraph, and the printing press combined – raised his advertising budget off Holloway's back. In Montreal, large columns of newspapers were purchased to direct invalids to his address in New York. 'Let us Reason Together', the headlines yelled. 'Why are we Sick?'

Sickness wasn't the half of it. In addition to Thomas's usual list of sore knees, female ailments and rheumatism, the American ointment bearing his name promised to come in handy in case of sabre cuts, gunshot wounds and steam explosions. Both the British and French armed forces officially endorsed Holloway's pills and ointment as the only failsafe method of reviving battered troops. Or so Haydock said. Indeed, a sensible soldier would reject the medicine offered by an army surgeon and demand Holloway's pills. Even the world's most despotic governments had opened their arms to these miraculous remedies. It truly was a triumph of medical science over human suffering.

CAUTION! None are genuine unless the words 'Holloway, New York, and London' are discernible as a watermark … a handsome reward will be given to any one rendering such information as may lead to the detection of any party or parties counterfeiting the medicines, or vending the same, knowing them to be spurious.

Of course, it was all bunkum. But bunkum that made money. Thomas's estimation of $100,000 in lost profits probably wasn't far off. Joseph Haydock was using Thomas's own advertising tactics against him, wooing the American family along with the thousands of walking wounded left over from the Civil War. Thomas published a lengthy damnation of his former agent in the American press, as Albinolo once had.

The *Chemist & Druggist* printed the final outcome in 1881:

Holloway's Medicines in America. – On 8 October Thos. Holloway, proprietor of Holloway's Pills and Ointment, obtained an injunction against Joseph Haydock, of New York, restraining him from manufacturing or selling the above articles, and especially from using Holloway's name. The injunction was violated by Haydock, and Holloway procured his prosecution for contempt of court. Under this prosecution Haydock was arrested and committed to gaol on the 3rd of November.

The news item preceding this was the sobering case of a James W. Tealc dying after taking his own Fever and Ague Cure, a nostrum riddled with arsenic. The *Chemist & Druggist* were amused. 'This is a remarkable case from the fact that it records the only known instance of a patent medicine man's having the temerity to take his own compound.' One more quack was behind bars, and another beneath the sod, but the industry rolled on uninterrupted.

For Haydock, it was fun while it lasted. However, his wasn't the sole American enterprise making money from Thomas's name. While Haydock's bogus advertisements cropped up all over the North American press, family almanacs were gracing the kitchens of ordinary American citizens, lavishly decorated and bearing in playbill script the name 'Johnston, Holloway & co'.

In Britain, Thomas had already produced his own Holloway Almanacs, packed with questionable advice on how to deal with sunstroke and other ailments. Most of these remedies unsurprisingly involve downing a handful of pills and then running to the privy. The medieval principal of the four humours was at work in these almanacs, particularly aimed at the foreign market where hot weather put the humours at special risk of imbalance. His advice for Australian customers, titled 'Health and Cheerfulness, Philosophy

1874.

HOOFLAND'S ALMANAC AND FAMILY RECEIPT BOOK FOR EVERYBODY'S USE.

JOHNSTON, HOLLOWAY & CO.,
No. 602 Arch Street, Philadelphia, Pa.,
PROPRIETORS OF
Hoofland's German Medicines.

Entered according to Act of Congress, in the year 1873, by JOHNSTON, HOLLOWAY & CO., Philada., in the Office of the Librarian of Congress at Washington.

30. Pretty and useful, family almanacs brought advertising into the home.
(Verity Holloway)

and Fact', relies on the failsafe, unsavory method beloved of quacks: emotional manipulation.

> It is not generally known, but such is the fact that children require medicine oftener than their parents. Three-fourths of the children die before they attain the age of eight years. Let their mothers, then, be wise, and give to their children small doses of these invaluable pills once or twice every week … The gross humors [*sic*] that are constantly floating about in the blood of children, the forerunners of so many complaints, will thus be expelled, and the lives of thousands saved and preserved to their parents.

Cheap, small, and readily available, family almanacs were a valuable advertising tool for the Victorian businessman. The culture of the self-reliant housewife meant almost every household had a medical handbook as the first port of call in cases of minor illness and injuries. Most contained recipes, calendars and jokes, alongside puff pieces pushing the publisher's products, promoting the company as family friendly and trustworthy. Why risk the pain and expense of a physician, when the almanac in the kitchen promised the Holloway mantra of 'health for all'?

Meanwhile, in Philadelphia, one Hiram C. Johnston had teamed up with a William Holloway to produce their own family almanac. A druggist and small-time doctor respectively, Johnston and William Holloway partnered in the early 1850s with James Cowden, who had experience in the patent medicine trade. The team acquired an existing herbal remedy, rebranding it as Hoofland's German Bitters and adding an epic backstory. Christoph Wilhelm Hoofland, they wrote, was one of the most renowned physicians of the modern age, earning fame for his proficiency in the art of prolonging life. Hoofland – or rather, Hufeland – was a real German physician whose book of household medicine was hugely popular in Europe during the 1700s. Despite Hoofland dying in 1836, Johnston and company claimed that Hoofland personally passed on his miracle cure to the American market in the 1850s via a Dr C.M. Jackson, who passed it on in 1863 to Johnston and Holloway.

> It has performed hundreds and thousands of the most astonishing cures, and its reputation and sale have now reached a point that far surpasses any remedy of the present or past ages. It has acquired this great reputation, not by a system of puffing, but by the actual merit of the article itself.

But Jackson, Johnson and William Holloway were not the only quacks pedalling a remedy named after the venerable Hufeland. A Swede by birth, Charles Roback lived an itinerant American life, passing from city to city making money by charging people to look at a baby alligator in a tin box, which he claimed was a crocodile he captured on an African adventure. In a rented office, Roback practised witchcraft for a fee, casting out demons, locating lost objects, and weaving love spells. He had already mastered the art of the newspaper puff piece for his dark arts, so it's no surprise he also dabbled in the patent medicine trade. With his European connections, it was easy to pass a German friend off as Hufeland's grandson and pedal the 'true' remedy. Adding to that stories of an ancestral castle, and grand titles in secret magical societies in London and St Petersburg, Roback charmed and astonished the people of Philadelphia with ease. The proprietors of Hoofland's German Bitters – also based in Philadelphia – were not so pleased. It wasn't easy to compete with a magi, particularly when both parties were telling the same lie.

But Johnston and Co had something Roback did not: William Holloway's name. After Roback appeared on the scene, benefiting from the Johnston company's advertising of Hoofland's Bitters in much the way Thomas Holloway's own brother attempted to benefit from his, the elegant Johnston premises on Philadephia's Arch Street underwent a makeover. Previously vivid pink with the Hoofland brand emblazoned on the side, the building was given six huge banners travelling the full width of each five storeys – 'FAMILY MEDICINE DEPOT, HOLLOWAY'S ARNICA PLASTERS, HEISKELLS TETTER OINTMENT, HOLLOWAY'S VERMIFUGE CONFECTIONS'.

If Roback could profit from someone else's labour, so could Johnston, Holloway & Co. Perhaps they noticed the Haydock newspaper fraud and thought to try their luck. It could have been a coincidence that the American Dr Holloway's astounding cure brought invalids from the verge of the grave – almost precisely the words Professor Holloway had used in Britain. In fact, a great deal of Thomas's wording and imagery found its way to Philadelphia.

Throughout the 1870s, *Hoofland's Almanac* helped American housewives create the perfect Christmas pudding, discover their zodiac sign, and lance a boil. These small magazines are a quaint and sometimes baffling insight into patent medicine as it appeared in everyday nineteenth-century life. Homeopathic cures for rabies and resuscitation methods for the drowned sit alongside recipes for pickled cauliflower and moral aphorisms warning against laziness. The 1874 edition contains several pages of letters in praise of various products masquerading as Holloway's, including a worm remedy, arnica plasters ('this is no quack preparation') and Jamaican ginger tonic for pep. Holloway's vermifuge tonic moved the public to write testimonials about their own tummy troubles in intimate detail. George Boyd of Filbert Street took the time to count forty-eight worms expelled from his toddler. 'The country people are running for them,' wrote a druggist from Milton, echoing the ad, which claims, rather dubiously, 'children crave them.'

The use of testimonials, coupled with the layout, and the format of the advertising, is recognisably copied from Thomas Holloway. Images of wise old sages in togas approached by needy travellers are almost identical. Thomas himself drew the line at using adorable cherubs carrying banners extolling the virtues of laxatives, but the American imitation bears a notable resemblance to *Punch's* 'Puff Pantomime' parody. From the Americans' point of view, the fraud

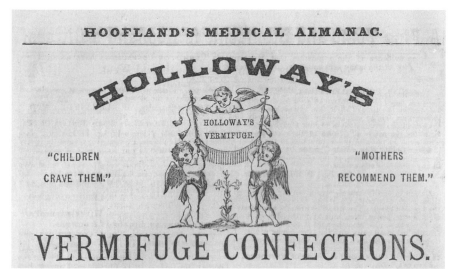

31. 'Children crave them', a counterfeit Holloway ad.
(Verity Holloway)

must have been too tempting to resist. If William Holloway was indeed the doctor's real name, the company would be silly not to use it, and arguably no laws had been broken – plausible deniability was on their side. A settler from Europe would likely not know this Philadelphian Holloway from the Cornish original, much as a German-speaking stranger could show up in town pretending to know the true recipe of Doctor Hufeland's medicine. German immigrants were very fond of Hoofland's Bitters, whoever was making them. The same could be said for Holloway's Pills and Ointment. And as Thomas was making no serious effort to break into America with his own products, he only had himself to blame.

'Caution,' wrote the Philadelphians. 'The unprecedented popularity of this VERMIFUGE has induced a great many unprincipled persons, all over the country, and even in Canada, to counterfeit and imitate them. Some of these preparations are of a dangerous character – containing calomel and other drastic drugs.'

For the quack doctor, the competitor was always the *real* quack. In this case. Johnston. Holloway & Co were keen to impress upon

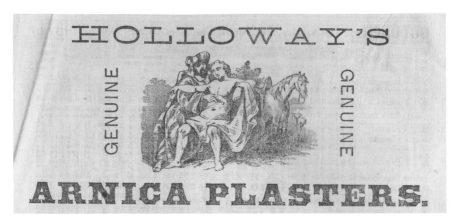

32. Another counterfeit Holloway ad. Arnica remains a popular herbal remedy for bruises, but has been shown to be no more potent than a placebo.
(Verity Holloway)

the public the safety of their wares, but their principles – like those of magi-for-hire Roback – in other areas were flimsier. 'Not a rum drink but a highly concentrated vegetable tonic,' goes one advertisement for their bitters. 'It is a Pure Medicinal Bitter, not alcoholic.' On examination, the bitters were found to be 25 per cent alcohol. This, too, was a deliberate and clever lie. The temperance movement in America could be equally, if not more, intense than its British cousin, and because of pressure from lobbying groups and individuals, druggists were moved to offer 'temperance drinks' to help working men enjoy a clandestine tipple without earning the wrath of wife or employer. Hoofland's was one of these, ostensibly a healthy pick-me-up containing no harmful stimulants whatsoever. 'Contains no alcohol' was, effectively, code for 'drink me', making them popular with well-to-do elderly ladies and other secretive drunks. Colden's Liquid Beef Tonic, 'recommended for treatment of alcohol habit', was 26.5 per cent alcohol. Another was found to contain a staggering 42 per cent. Preachers were paid to advocate the bitters, which claimed to cure 'Constant Imaginings of Evil' in the way only a stiff drink can. The patent medicine trade was built upon layers of lies.

No one could deny that Holloway's Pills and Ointment were known the world over. Of course, if the Philadelphian counterfeits proved to be dangerous, the Americans had the advantage of passing the blame to the real Holloway and continuing business with the same product under another name. It is worth mentioning that the company were also producing 'chill pills', popular cold remedies sometimes containing arsenous acid, also known as rat poison. Thomas's medicines had already been implicated in a murder case in Ireland, although the verdict was clear there was nothing in the pills to cause death, or even injury. By leaving a gap in the American market, he had unwittingly left his own reputation open to attack.

Thomas's correspondence at the time shows he was all too conscious of people willing to maliciously profit from his business. Mr Rough – the rogue who spent his wages on drink – had emerged from Thomas's telling-off with plans for revenge. Evidently new to skulduggery, he made the unwise decision to put his threats in writing. Wearily disappointed, Thomas responded:

Dear Sir,
I have no desire to hurt your feelings more than by a mere allusion to the threat which you made to me that you would go immediately to New York; & as this threat of yours, I presume, hardly appeared strong enough for your purpose, you sent to Oxford Street the same evening a letter, which I have here, to the effect that you were in correspondence with a party who need not be named – & you came into the office & went to your desk & took out a packet of my letters which you put in your pocket. I say nothing of your most unaccountable absence for several days from your duties at the office – no one I am sure would say other than your conduct was such as could not be excused – if taken into consideration that I gave you no cause whatever for such treatment but on the contrary I have I believe always treated you with kindness.

Could Rough have been in league with Haydock? The timing was right, and Haydock was clearly well informed, even after officially cutting ties with his employer. Rough had motive, having already received a humiliating telling off from Holloway on the orders of his own wife. The issue of his drinking habits had been hanging over the office, making him unpopular with his colleagues. Perhaps Thomas had nagged. He certainly took the opportunity to use Rough's past behaviour as a stick to beat him with once more:

> Men who will treat their wives & their own flesh & blood as you have done would not be unlikely, if they had a chance, by which they could benefit themselves to bring trouble upon their employers.
>
> It was not my intention to have referred to the letter of Mrs Rough but I do so for the purpose of acquainting you that there is strong feeling manifested by all the clerks in the office against you – in consequence of your heartless conduct. I am sorry I cannot call it by a milder name.

Thomas ends by reassuring Rough that a young man of his talents always has time to turn his life around, and that he had no intention of taking action upon Rough's foolhardy threats. It was more kindness than Rough deserved, and indeed, had Thomas been younger, his temper would almost certainly have been roused. It was likely only the thought of Rough's pale children that stopped Thomas from summoning his lawyer.

The passion was strangely lacking. The offices, built with such pride and furnished with every amenity a visitor could wish for, had once delighted the press and cemented Holloway as an esteemed household brand. The thought of a trusted colleague sneaking through desks and stealing paperwork would surely have enraged the most genial of employers. But Thomas had more serious matters to dwell on. His sister, Matilda, had died suddenly at the age of fifty-four, necessitating the purchase of a family plot at St Michael and All Angels in Sunninghill. She was the first of the Holloway siblings to die, and her monument would one day be Thomas's too, and Jane's. Where once Thomas would have taken Rough to task for his terrible behaviour, the older, wiser Thomas knew the value of forgiveness.

Another explanation for his lacklustre attitude during this episode was that financially there was no need to carry on with pills and ointment. Indeed, Thomas had been working to rid himself of these disreputable ties, turning instead to property investment and the lucrative import of Australian wool. These investments were making far more revenue than his remedies. Perhaps he had been intending to slowly back out of the patent medicine business, until Haydock and others had interfered with the Holloway name. It is all too likely the fraud was forcing Thomas to examine his own beginnings with Albinolo, and how he had prospered where his partner had faded into obscurity. It was around this time that the eccentric little Italian of Soho died. Perhaps guilt was playing on his mind.

A hundred thousand dollars' worth of trouble or not, money was not the crux of the American problem. Thomas had set up his own Holloway Bank with the profits from his shrewd property investments and stocks. So vast were these sums, he made a loan to the French government to aid in their war against the Prussians. In his investments, we see how truly shrewd Thomas was with money. While he sat at home, quietly watering down his wine with Jane, the Holloway riches were ploughed into shares in a huge variety of international endeavours: Brazilian underwater telegraph systems, the Indian peninsular railways, debentures in Alabama, Texas and New Orleans, and loans to the Mexican government. His boast of correspondences with kings around the world wasn't entirely in jest. Pills and ointment were really only one facet of a complex and clever series of business ventures that set Thomas apart from his contemporary patent medicine manufacturers. It wasn't surprising, then, that during the 1870s, he dropped the 'Professor'. It had always been rather too brash a title.

Competitors were moving in on the home front, too. Twenty years Holloway's junior was Thomas Beecham, one of seven children of poor parents in Oxfordshire. Beecham was a farmer's boy who spent ten years working seven-day weeks in the fields. It was there that he learned herb lore from the country folk and took to mixing his own teas and simple remedies, which he sold at market. Beecham and Holloway came into business about the same time. In 1847, Beecham acquired a licence permitting him to sell medicines, and wasted no time marketing his Female's Friends, Golden Tooth Tincture, Royal Toothpowder and Beecham's Pills, which, curiously enough, were largely aloe flavoured with ginger, the same as Holloway's Pills. Beecham essentially began his career as a mountebank, travelling from market to market, before finding instant success with a mail order service. To keep up with demand, he was forced to move again and again to larger buildings, eventually settling in industrial Lancashire with a factory of his own. Beecham successfully took pre-Industrial Revolution folk cures and put them on the modern production line. 'Worth a Guinea a box', Beecham's Pills were shipped to Africa and Australia, with print advertisements in all the same papers as Holloway's Pills. A total of 14,000 international papers featured testimonials from men and women all over the world, relieved to be back in the pink of health thanks to these wonderful pills that 'made life worth living'. The placebo effect was to thank for much of Beecham's success, but like Holloway's pills, the bowel-loosening power of the aloe was a deliberate trick to keep customers coming back to this effective remedy. It all sounds strikingly familiar, even down to the popular gag of faking a dramatic choking spasm before getting up, brushing oneself down, and declaring, 'Why, if I hadn't had nineteen Beecham's Pills this morning, I'd be dead now!'

Beecham was altogether a younger model of Holloway. Where Holloway employed scores of young women to pack pill boxes by hand, Beecham left such repetitive (not to mention unhygienic) work to modern machinery. Holloway's old shop at the end of the Strand had been too cluttered to introduce steam-powered assembly lines of any sort, and the Oxford Street shop was too ornate. This failure to adopt modern technology resulted in pills that were irregular in shape and size, and therefore dosage. Beecham's pills, on the other hand, were reassuringly uniform, thanks to steam-powered automation. Holloway was unconcerned with quality control – why should he have been, when the most successful quacks of the past had whipped up concoctions on the spot? – but this was a mistake. As the 1870s went on, pharmaceuticals were erring more on the side of science, not magic, and the public were coming to expect a more clinical approach.

So too was Beecham tapping into the subtly changing advertising scene. Where Holloway's advertisements were solemn and stuffily Victorian in tone, Beecham utilised humour with cute cartoons and clever visual jokes, directing their focus at a younger market of families and the upwardly mobile workers of the cities. Beecham knew the grandparents of these potential customers were likely fond of the herbal country remedies he learnt as a boy, lending his pills a familiar trustworthy quality, but also required more modern marketing. As Thomas J. Barratt, father of the cutesy Pears' Soap advertisements that dominated the turn of the century, rightly noted: 'Tastes change, fashions change, and the advertiser has to change with them. An idea that was effective a generation ago would fall flat, stale and unprofitable if presented to the public today.' Mighty professors and miracle workers were slowly becoming old hat. Truth, obviously, didn't come into the equation, but down-to-earth authenticity, with a dash of popular culture, was gradually coming into favour with the market. Beecham was savvy enough to nod to celebrities and trends of the day, paraphrasing music hall songs and even the words of Charles Dickens (who was, by then, too dead to protest). Henry Irving, the giant of the Victorian stage, appears as Hamlet in one advertisement: 'To Beecham or not to Beecham? Methinks I've heard they are worth a guinea a box.'

Beecham, Holloway had doubtless realised, was an up-to-date version of himself. Oddly, both Thomases married women called Jane, but unlike Holloway, Beecham produced heirs who were

33. Beecham's Pills were almost identical to Holloway's.
(Wellcome Library, London)

already lending a hand to the family business by the time Holloway was well past having any children of his own. Worse, Holloway's own dear Jane was in decline. 'Grace Darling' was succumbing to chills and coughs no amount of medicine could shift. It seemed unfair that a woman so many years his junior looked increasingly likely to leave him a widow. With this painful knowledge, Thomas put his energy not only into protecting his legacy, but building it further than his critics could ever foresee.

America needed immediate forceful action. The Civil War had given the fake Holloway plenty of fodder for getting his foot into the door. Beautiful coloured ads show foreign soldiers in classical poses, dressing wounds with a single white pot of ointment. Another is taken straight from the popular melodramas of the day, and more recognisably political, with a Union soldier dashing to his fallen comrade, a box of Holloway's Pills in hand.

> TO ARMS! TO ARMS!! The citizen solider will find a more deadly foe in the brackish muddy water and damp night air, than in the most determined enemy.

Luckily, Haydock had not decided to print Holloway ads supporting the losing Confederates. Nevertheless, in the four years America was at war with herself, around 200,000 soldiers succumbed to disease. Thomas enlisted the help of his sister Mary Jane and her husband Philip Hutchings, who were planning to relocate across the Atlantic. They were despatched to make wholesale contacts, utilising every trick that had worked in Britain, plus using Haydock's legwork as a stepping stone on the way to crushing him. Over the following years, the real Holloway company rolled out an enormous print campaign, product placement in plays and music halls, cigarette cards and patriotic ephemera. Prints were produced to distribute all over the fraudsters' territory and beyond, depicting Holloway's Pills in every corner of the globe. Beautifully drawn men and women appear with bright turbans, gossamer veils and outlandish

34. Attempting to update the company's image, Thomas created eye-catching trade cards of international customs. On the reverse, Holloway's Pills are proclaimed a British institution.
(Wellcome Library, London)

exotic hairstyles, posing like models in fashion plates, making them eye-catching and instantly collectable.

The message to his competitors was clear – Holloway, like the British Empire, had already conquered the world. Looking back on his youth, Thomas wrote, 'early impressions make an indelible mark on the mind, that no time or circumstance can obliterate.' Quiet though he may have been, he had always been a man to stride out into the world and get what he wanted. Old age would not curtail him.

The college and the sanatorium were on their way to completion. Neither Beecham nor the American fraudsters could touch achievements of that magnitude, and yet Thomas looked at their splendour and saw a glaring gap. Another gift to the nation was in order, and Thomas's personal papers, collected after his death, give a glimpse of his state of mind during the trying 1870s, and the peculiar obsession that may have fuelled this final ambition.

Chapter 12

Man Proposes, God Disposes

'That able navigator, Sir John Franklin, is about again to proceed on a Polar expedition, having under his orders the *Erebus* and *Terror*, which are preparing for this arduous service.' So announced The *Brighton Gazette* on Thursday, 13 February 1845.

Balding, portly, and possessing a mighty pair of mid-Victorian sideboards, Sir John Franklin looked more like a banker than an intrepid explorer. By his twenties, he already had an impressive portfolio of successful sea battles and expeditions under his belt, including surviving the Battle of Trafalgar aboard the HMS *Bellerophon*. Coincidentally, the *Bellerophon* had fought in the 'Glorious First of June' battle with France, which Thomas Holloway senior took part in. Thomas retained a lifelong interest in his father's brief time in combat, so perhaps this tenuous family link was what prompted him to pay special attention to the 1845 voyage of Sir Franklin. Over the following decades, Thomas amassed clippings from his collection of international newspapers – said to be the most comprehensive in Britain – charting the Polar expedition and the subsequent events that gripped Victorian Britain.

For centuries, ships from various nations had gone in search of the fabled Northwest Passage through the Arctic, linking the Atlantic Ocean to the Pacific. For a trading empire like Britain, discovering such a shortcut from Europe to Asia would mean huge gains, not to mention prestige. During the first half of the nineteenth century, there had already been several British attempts to find the Northwest Passage, by sea and overland. One of the most successful of these was that of Rear Admiral William Parry in 1819, aboard the HMS *Hecla*, accompanied by HMS *Griper*. Both ships were equipped with incredibly thick hulls for icebreaking, cork insulation, and plentiful supplies of the new invention of tinned rations, which kept out beetles and all but the most persistent and deft of crew members – tin openers had yet to be invented.

Early nineteenth-century theories of disease governed the crews' dress. As the ever-useful Holloway's *Medical Guide for the use of missionaries* pointed out:

> To the missionary, traveller, and settler, it is of unspeakable importance to be possessed of such medical knowledge as will enable him to deal successfully with such diseases as mostly prevail, or are endemic in different climates and countries ... Nature has furnished the human organism with a vital fluid – the Blood – on which the healthy or unhealthy condition of which depends the health, nay, even life itself.

For the health of the blood, sudden changes in temperature were considered deadlier than continual cold or heat, hence every anxious grandmother's stock phrase, 'You'll catch a chill'. Therefore, Polar explorers, constantly having to switch between ice-swept decks and sweaty furnace rooms, were equipped with that most Victorian of garments – woollen combination underwear. For the Arctic, a woollen vest and pair of drawers sounds perfectly reasonable, but this theory of temperature change meant Victorian explorers heading to the Tropics also had their crews kitted out with 'woollies'. The idea was to insulate the blood from sudden blasts of heat, so alien to British flesh. In 1823, the crew of HMS *Valorous* had only just completed a chilly tour of the Labradorean coast before setting sail again for the West Indies. Still swaddled in their woollen undergarments, not a single man died during the voyage – a record the captain attributed to wool. Although the theory of heat changes was not exactly scientifically sound, wool's porous nature drew sweat away from the skin, gently cooling it in heat and insulating it in the cold.

Bunkum though Holloway's advice for travellers was, it appeared to work. The medieval theory of balancing the humours remained a staple of seafaring life well into the twentieth century. It's little wonder that individual sailors each had their own favourite patent medicine to swear by, as so many – Holloway's included – promised to work on the bodily fluids before disease had a chance to take hold.

The unusually warm weather of 1819 allowed Parry's crews to enter the icy seas with relatively little trouble. But surviving the cold was only one of their challenges. As expected, the ships were frozen in for ten months. Ten months of unbroken darkness quickly got to work on the men's minds. But Parry was a resourceful captain, and had the men compiling a weekly newspaper, as well as putting on small plays to pass the time and keep morale as high as possible. Inevitably, scurvy broke out. Teeth dropped out and old wounds reopened, but Parry had wisely used the last of the daylight to grow cress in his cabin. The tiny leaves helped stave off the worst of the symptoms, and incredibly, only one man died. Despite the ships only managing to get halfway across the Arctic, the crew returned home to fame and fortune, with a publisher purchasing Parry's memoirs for a thousand guineas.

With that kind of money at stake, it's easy to see why so many crews were willing to risk the journey into uncharted waters. These continual expeditions usually began with prospective captains surveying the previous crew's route and deciding that they would almost have made it, were it not for a single mistake.

Sir John Franklin estimated there were only another 500 kilometers of unexplored ice between him and the discovery of the fabled Northwest Passage. All that needed to be done was to wait out the winter months iced in, as Parry had, before pushing on. Franklin already had a reputation as a slightly mad but determined explorer, with valuable experience of inclement frozen terrain. Charting the coast of Canada overland from Hudson Bay to the mouth of Coppermine River, Franklin had fallen into the frozen river and been carried downstream to what would have been certain death had his crew not chased him down and hauled him out. It was an omen for the rest of the expedition, which descended into starvation, paranoia and murder. Eleven out of the twenty-strong group did not survive. Starvation has a powerful effect on the mind. In the suffocating fog, the men were forced to subsist on their own shoe leather, gaining Franklin the nickname 'the man who eats his boots'. And there was worse to come:

> The officer and men had come down to the point of actual starvation, beyond even the stage where they were feeding upon rotten offal which excoriated their mouths; and they were without a thought of recourse to a sustenance which is worse than death. But there was one amongst them – Michel, a Canadian – who frequently absented himself in the rear; who took possession of a hatchet under circumstances which suggested that he intended to cut up something frozen; and who remained strong ... This Michel once brought some piece of meat which he asserted to be wolf's flesh, but which, there was afterwards reason to suspect, was part of a fellow Canadian ... Richardson undertook the responsibility of shooting him.

Such a hideous debacle may have given the government pause, but did not prevent them giving Franklin two lavishly equipped ships, the HMS *Erebus* and *Terror*. The ships departed in June. Early accounts sent home said the crews were in high spirits and optimistic that the ice would open up and allow them westward. They had supplies for up to four years, including thousands of tinned rations, and the ships were specifically designed to cope with thick ice; state of the art vessels built with the strongest wood and iron available. The papers painted the explorers as true British heroes, and the public lapped it up. No officer was more suited to the task, or more familiar with the Arctic, they said, than Franklin. It was a most admirable expedition, an example of the intrepid British spirit, and had every chance of succeeding. Like everyone else, Thomas Holloway followed news of the voyage with interest. Recent finds by archaeologists show the crews carried patent

35. Sir John Franklin. Stipple engraving by D.J. Pound, 1860, after M. Negelen.
(Wellcome Library, Images)

medicine with them on their voyage. It would have been a great boon for Holloway's Pills, of course, had he persuaded Franklin to put in a good word for him in the press, but in 1845, Thomas was barely a blip on the patent medicine market. Indeed, considering what was to come, that was probably a blessing.

Sometime in the following year, both HMS *Erebus* and HMS *Terror* vanished. Rumours came from Greenland that the ships were weathering their second winter in a safe haven, perhaps Gilbert's Sound, but the last whaler of the season returned home without having seen signs of either ship, or their crews. The papers held their breath. The ice, they noted, was setting in with unusual severity.

£20,000 REWARD will be given by Her Majesty's Government to any party, or parties, of any country, who shall render efficient assistance to the crews of the discovery ships under the command of Sir John Franklin.

In 1847, a search party was sent out. The winter had forced them to wait longer than was ideal, but hopes were high that the ships were safe. Hermetically sealed metal tubes were on board the *Erebus* and the *Terror*, ready to contain despatches to be tossed overboard and picked up by vessels navigating the North Sea. When none of the tubes surfaced as expected, the newspapers were quick to cover the search effort. All over the country, Sir Franklin and his men were referred to as gallant explorers in peril, a band of adventurers, giving the whole affair the feeling of the heroic fiction devoured by British schoolboys. Other papers were more cautious, publishing a letter from Sir Franklin to Colonel Sabine concerning his possible late return:

> I hope my dear wife and daughter will not be over anxious if we should not return by the time they may have fixed upon; and I must beg of you to give them the benefit of your advice and experience when that arrives, for you know well that even after the second winter, without success in our object, we should wish to try some other channel if the state of our provisions and the health of the crews justify it.

But the public was nervous. Rumours of a fresh search party – on land, this time, in case the ships had foundered – were already flying, despite attempts to cover it up. Sir John Ross, who had already led two Polar expeditions and been knighted for his efforts, volunteered to follow Franklin's path. Coverage of the Polar expedition grew from a few short lines to lengthy articles syndicated nationally.

'On these expeditions it is not too much to say, the eyes of the civilised world are now fixed with most intense interest.'

By December 1849, the rescue effort was a forlorn hope. Coverage of the search parties' expeditions was still published widely, detailing every possible minutiae for the interested public, as though they at home could somehow help to find the gallant crew. Optimistic pieces talked about how unlikely starvation was, with the Canadian Arctic offering all kinds of plants and animals to sustain Sir Franklin and his men. But such theories were filler, and most readers knew it.

Lady Franklin offered a substantial reward for a successful search party. An air balloon search of the Arctic was proposed, but deemed too likely to require a rescue party of its own. Instead, Lady Franklin had watertight cylinders bearing letters scattered about the Canadian Arctic for other ships to find, and a high pole constructed to attract the attention of any wandering crew members. Another rescue crew captured Arctic foxes and released them with collars bearing messages hammered into copper. The most bizarre – and most Victorian – of these rescue attempts was that of Mrs Haddock of Bolton, a clairvoyant who offered her services to survey the Arctic via psychic remote viewing.

In a trance state, Mrs Haddock claimed Franklin was still alive, but the ships were stranded on the ice, awaiting rescue. After one or two minor nautical inaccuracies, her husband was moved to publish a letter in the press explaining that because of 'her comparative removal from the influence of the laws of space and time, we must expect to find many anachronisms and incongruities in her statements, similar to what we all experience in ordinary dreams.' As the clairvoyant was unable to read or write, said her supporters, her supernatural ability to decipher maps shown to her by Sir Franklin was deserving of respect. Sir Franklin's friends at the Admiralty ought to take heart from Mrs Haddock's visions, said her husband, and indeed they did, requesting a further interview. Passing into a trance state with a deep sigh, Mrs Haddock commented that she enjoyed speaking to Sir Franklin, but that his would-be rescuer, Sir James Ross, was grumpy, uncommunicative, and – apparently importantly – bald. (For the sake of Sir Ross's posthumous honour, he did in fact have a full head of hair at the time.)

'Dear me!' the *Northampton Echo* reported Mrs Haddock exclaiming. 'What heaps of snow, they are higher than I ever saw them! Oh, how cold it is!' Animals were abundant, including leaping snow tigers and forests teeming with wild cattle. She went on to say she herself would prefer to starve to death than consume the alcohol the crew were partial to, but worse were the natives' habit of eating raw fish while dancing around in animal skins. Sir Franklin, she commented, had plenty of food in thick metal tins.

The press loved this. The *Leicester Journal* particularly enjoyed Mrs Haddock's remark that so much money had been wasted in attempting to locate the missing ships. 'What indeed, since by a few mesmeric strokes all the information can be procured, without a single cockboat leaving our shores!'

Over the following decades, mentions of the missing crew appeared in small paragraphs alongside novelty pieces about Siamese twins and local mesmerism societies. Rescue parties interviewed the indigenous Inuits (referred to as 'Esquimaus' in the British press) who spoke of ships trapped in ice, a battle for weapons, and the discovery of human bones bearing signs of flesh removal. Being the words of foreigners, they were automatically discounted. Charles Dickens called the Inuits 'a race of savages', likely to have killed the crew themselves. Not everyone was so outraged. Those who knew Franklin's history were all too aware that cannibalism was a very real last resort.

And then, a breakthrough. In the Arctic, a note was discovered pinned by rocks and snow: 'Sir John Franklin commanding the Expedition. All well.' The note was dated 28 May 1847. In the margins, however, another message told a different story. Dated 25 April 1848, it described the two periods of wintering ashore, as had always been expected. But the ships had been trapped in the ice far longer than anyone could have anticipated – a year and a half passed. Two weeks after the 'all well' note, disease broke out

– most likely tuberculosis, made worse by scurvy when supplies dwindled. Sir Franklin died, along with twenty-four crewmembers, and the survivors chose to abandon their ships in search of supplies. Soon, the ships succumbed to the crushing ice and sunk, leaving no trace. The note was dotted with drops of what looked like blood. Between the cold, the starvation, and disease, there was little hope of finding survivors.

Grim discoveries trickled in over the following years. In 1859, two bodies were found sitting in a lifeboat on the shore, as if waiting for rescue. Bodies continued to be discovered up until the 1990s, scattered about in the permafrost, having fallen while walking. The mummified remains of three crew members discovered in the 1980s showed the men suffered from lead poisoning contracted from the thick metal food tins Mrs Haddock saw in her visions. The tins had been manufactured in haste, and inexpertly soldered so that lead leaked into the food. The level of poison present in the bodies was severe enough to cause severe physical and mental breakdowns, including aggression and memory loss. The crew were doomed from the moment they set off. What the Inuits said about white men with guns running wild was most likely accurate, but there was worse to come. Some of the bodies displayed cut marks consistent with butchery.

Despite all of the evidence that the crew turned on each other in the desperation to survive, the Victorian press still hailed Franklin and his men as heroes. Songs were written, plays performed, and statues erected to the memory of the explorers' bravery. Poet Algernon Charles Swinburne penned an elegy summing up the nation's grief and pride, but also the desire to turn ugly events into something glorious:

> High honour shall they have; their deeds shall make
> Their spoken names sound sweeter than all song.
> This England hath not made a better man,
> More steadfast, or more wholly pure of wrong
> Since the large book of English praise began.

Thomas Holloway added each new report to his collection. Alone in his study at Tittenhurst, he had amassed a blow-by-blow account of high ambition gone foul, watching as the tragedy became legend within his lifetime. The story resonated with Thomas, but the saccharine tributes clashed with his natural melancholy. As the son of a seafarer, and having grown up around sailors, he doubtless knew the atrocities that went on at sea. The story of Owen Coffin and the crew of the American whaling ship *Essex* had rocked 1820s Britain. When the whale they were pursuing turned on the ship and sunk it, the surviving crew piled into lifeboats with enough provisions to live on for two months. The *Essex* had sunk some 3,000 kilometres off the west coast of South Africa, and what with their food supplies having been soaked in seawater, men quickly began to die. The situation became so desperate, not only did the survivors resort to eating the bodies of the dead, they drew lots on who should be sacrificed to keep the rest alive. Seventeen-year-old Owen Coffin resigned himself to his fate, and was shot by his crewmates. When one of the lifeboats was discovered, the emaciated survivors were still clutching his bones. The American and British public were horrified, but long-time seafarers knew perfectly well how quickly men abandon their principles in the face of death. The *Essex* crews' memoirs went on to inspire *Moby Dick*, a far grimmer portrayal of the madness of the sea than perhaps the public would have liked.

For Thomas Holloway, the Franklin expedition was a disaster that struck a chord. This dark fixation stayed with him from the very start of his career until the twilight years of his life; a total of nearly forty years. The sanatorium and the college cemented the Holloway name as a Victorian institution, but these victories brought strangely little joy. Taciturn as Thomas was on the subject of his personal life, his fascination with the Franklin expedition and its cultural fallout took his life in one last unexpected direction.

Despite the impressive beauty of 'the two institutions', the 1870s were trying times for Thomas Holloway. George Martin,

Thomas's brother-in-law, was placed in charge of dealing with yet more fraud, this time in Switzerland and Austria. 'It becomes necessary for someone to be present in these countries to take the necessary proceedings for the suppression of the same,' Martin wrote to an acquaintance in need of employment. 'Now I know you are energetic and persevering – would you like to undertake such a Business?' Not so long ago, Thomas himself had been an energetic and persevering young man. But his interest in pills and ointment was waning, and challenges to his business were now more a tiring annoyance than a call to arms.

Thomas was sick at heart. George had to beg him to take interest in the European frauds – entanglements, Thomas called them, keeping him awake at night, unable to shift the little coughs and colds that were increasingly disrupting his schedule. Old friends were dying off. He and Jane spoke many times of a dear Cornish companion who seemed likely to outlive them all. His sudden death shook the Holloways, and they agreed to wipe out all his debts to them for the sake of his children.

Thomas had his own legacy on his mind. In March 1872, he wrote to an Anglican friend in Cornwall – Reverend Richard Tyacke – on the subject of 'the Boy Bennett'. Bennett was probably one of the eight children of James Bennett, a Cornish cousin of Thomas's who had died the previous year. Thomas and Jane were interested in the child's welfare, and desired he join in with the other Cornish boys in helping harvest the season's pilchards before being set up as an apprentice to learn a valuable trade. Mrs Tyacke had been badgering Thomas to help fund renovations to their church, and it appears she was using Bennett as a bargaining tool. The Tyackes were well off (the Reverend in fact opened his own golf club) and had many business contacts in Cornwall, but Mrs Tyacke hinted her family would only manage the boy's welfare if the church was invested in first. Thomas was not a lover of organised religion, nor was he a man to be nagged. In a second letter, Thomas renounced 'once & for all the intention I entertained of apprenticing the Boy'.

Life, as you very justly observe, is uncertain & I could not undertake
to encumber my executors with the responsibility of looking after
the boy until manhood … he must consequently take his chance
in life as his Eldest Brother has done before him … Be pleased to
assure Mrs Tyacke, as from me, my sense of deep obligation that
she was pleased to say she would attend to the boy's Clothing – to
you I am greatly indebted for all the trouble you have had & which
ends in nothing.

Was Bennett another unofficially adopted child, like Jane's niece,
Celia Martin? Thomas's lugubrious tone belies his and Jane's real
frustration. The couple were opening daily begging letters, a barrage
of pleas from distant acquaintances, and even strangers. 'I receive
too many appeals from the fair sex & they are such bold beggars
too,' Thomas told Reverend Tyacke.

Worse were his own kin: Cousin Willie was still carousing his
way through life, confident that a windfall was coming his way
when Thomas finally expired. Thomas was evidentially distressed
enough by Willie's behaviour that he got in contact with his
estranged brother Henry for advice. Having been in dire financial
straits himself, and gifted with a silver tongue, Henry was willing
to play messenger between Willie's irate employers and Thomas's
chequebook, though he was too proud to take money from Thomas
himself. Thomas had tried and failed to use his stock market
windfalls to rouse Henry into taking celebratory cash gifts. The
injunction still stood between the brothers.

Where once Thomas had hoped that doling out small chunks
of his fortune would drive a man to bigger and better things, it
was becoming all too clear to Thomas that being the rich uncle
invited cynical displays of neediness from those too lazy to make
their own way in life. But what was he to do, Thomas asked? If
he responded to a few worthy individuals, he would be accused
of favouritism. If he ignored them all, he would become a miser.
Charity, he still firmly believed, demeaned the recipient. The

Methodist Church got involved with Bennett's case, offering the boy a measly apprenticeship. Thomas, with his dislike of Methodists in general, found it galling, especially when the Tyackes themselves were Anglicans. Bennett's mother continued to pelt Tittenhurst with pleas for money over the following years, earning her one of George Martin's trademark sour letters:

> It would appear you and your husband have always been in trouble and could never help yourselves, so long as you could get money from here, and now it appears you have other troubles and so you always will have, and from what I know of your case, I should not advise Mr Holloway to give you any further assistance.

Not as hard as he tried to appear, Thomas authorised a £2 gift when Mrs Bennett's roof needed repairs. George pretended this was his doing, and that Mister Holloway was judiciously ignoring her, but the widow saw through him and continued to beg. In total, she squeezed over £300 from the Holloway coffers before George had the final word: 'Mister Holloway will have nothing more to do with you. You must support yourself as other poor people have to do.'

Thomas couldn't take the boy Bennett on as a ward without contending with the mother's constant hankering for funds. Saddened, he and Jane dropped the idea. 'As Shakespeare says,' he told Tyacke, 'it is "Loves labour lost".'

During the depressing 1870s, Thomas was looking for one last project to plough his fortune into. Something more worthy than Cornish churches and wastrel cousins. He wrote to Welby Pugin as the sanatorium neared completion: 'In my little way, I want to do something that coming generations may not, to use your expression, consider an incubus.' This increasing feeling of futility may well have been weighing on his mind the morning he opened *The Illustrated London News* to read the description of a shocking new painting:

Under the lurid sky of Arctic twilight, among the vast fantastic blocks of ice, green, or of livid pallor, save where faintly flushed with the long, level, rosy ray of the far-off dawn, we see over a hollow a solitary spar; and on the brink of this strange and awful grave – for those are human ribs protruding, blanched and bare from summer heat or birds of prey.

Edwin Henry Landseer was one of the nation's most beloved painters of animals. His depiction of a Newfoundland dog popularised the breed as a gallant rescuer of those in peril, and even his paintings of wild creatures somehow characterised animals as pure-hearted things, either devoted to mankind or offering an uncontaminated example of nobility to aspire to. Landseer offered a special brand of Victorian sentiment, and the public loved it. Queen Victoria was an admirer, commissioning the artist to immortalise her pets as well as her family. (Her Majesty found the man himself rather fetching, too, if a trifle short.) In 1867, the artist's most public work was installed in Trafalgar Square: four enormous bronze lions at the base of Nelson's Column. The scale of the project left Landseer with nightmares of being stalked by wild beasts.

But when the artist turned to the Franklin expedition for inspiration, something changed. The painting described in *The Illustrated London News* was neither noble nor sentimental. There had been painted tributes to the Franklin expedition before, far more to the public's taste, subtly hinting at tragedy only, with the sort of picturesque melancholy that could be consumed with enjoyment. Three years earlier, Frederic Edwin Church had unveiled his *Icebergs*, a candy-coloured Polar landscape with just a tip of a wrecked mast visible in the luminous foreground. The trouble with these sentimental works was that they offered no closure. There were those who still believed the crew would return, ragged yet victorious, like something from a boy's storybook. Landseer's bleak vision shocked because it told the harrowing truth. And then there was the title. Popularly known as *The Bears*, Landseer's own title was more disturbing: *Man Proposes, God Disposes*.

36. *Man Proposes, God Disposes*, 1864, oil on canvas, Edwin Landseer.
(©Royal Holloway, University of London)

Like the rest of the Victorian public, Landseer had been drawn along with the unfolding horrors of the Franklin expedition. But far from being moved to paint the disaster with the gloss of heroism, Landseer created a confrontational vision of futility, stark and bare. It was a modern *memento mori*, flying in the face of Victorian optimism and industry. This, coming from the man who created the lions guarding Nelson's Column – that enduring symbol of British power – was an unexpected slap of reality. Men and their little schemes were less than nothing, said the painting, and they needed to be reminded.

The work was far from a failure, drawing crowds to the Royal Academy's 1864 exhibition, and earned awed reactions from the press. *The Athenaeum* reviewer summed up the nation's discomfort. It was beautiful, haunting, but 'as to his choice of subject, we protest against it.'

Seen by most at the time as in poor taste (Lady Franklin, after all, was still alive), Landseer's friends blamed *Man Proposes* on the dark forces present in the painter's life. Landseer had been well on his way to a mental breakdown since 1840. Dependent on drugs and alcohol, he was declared insane in 1872 at the request of his family, and died the following year. The nation mourned. The bronze lions that had tormented him so were draped in black crepe, and flags were hung at half-mast for the man who so beautifully humanised animals. For the time being, the ghastly polar bears were forgotten.

Until they came on the market, that is. Art has always been a smart investment, as paintings accrue value and can be sold in times of need. Thomas Holloway was shrewd enough to take note when his fellow entrepreneurs were quietly selling their collections; a sure sign of weakness. Many eminent Victorian artists were less than delighted about the necessary evil of selling their works to businessmen interested only in resale value. When one such patron suggested Pre-Raphaelite Dante Gabriel Rossetti add a cheerful sunset over his painting to make it more commercial, Rossetti sent him packing.

Thomas was as guilty of art hoarding as anyone else with money to play with. In 1869, he happened upon Captain Joseph Dingwall on a train journey, and on impulse, made an offer on the Captain's Broomfield Hall. With it came seventy-eight paintings – mostly old masters, and little of personal interest to Thomas or Jane. Thomas was not an especially avid follower of the arts. Apart from occasional evenings with Jane at the theatre, and a normal interest in the big literary names of the day, he was far too dedicated to his work to spend much time outside the world of business. However, during his energetic tours of Europe, Thomas's diaries always recorded speedy visits to the local galleries for glimpses of the more famous paintings. Ballrooms of stately homes interested him when lined with pictures, and he took care to mention those he liked. Somewhat conservative of taste, he enjoyed Rubens, and Frith's modern vision of a bustling railway station, noting them down in the same matter-of-fact fashion with which he recorded his own weight and the day's weather. There was no indication in those days that he had interest in becoming a buyer for pleasure, rather than business.

It was during the trials of the mid-1870s that Thomas heard *Man Proposes, God Disposes* was on the market. While his competitors pecked at him from Europe, America, and home soil, he reflected on how fragile human accomplishments truly were. But the worst came on 26 September 1875.

Jane died of bronchitis. Only sixty-one, she had been weakening for some time, but her death was a sudden shock. Their marriage spanned forty years, enduring Thomas's gruelling work schedule, and the childlessness that clearly left a mark on them both. Jane had been with him since the difficult beginning, going with Thomas door to door with baskets of pills. Her family was closer to him than his own kin. Indeed, those near the Holloways said Thomas almost instantly adopted the Drivers, and their eagerness to take his surname proved a deep mutual affection. Jane was laid to rest in St Michael and All Angels Church, Sunninghill, alongside Matilda Holloway. A subdued memorial of salmon granite was erected to the affectionate memory of Thomas's beloved. No amount of patent medicine could have saved her. The former professor's own promises of miraculous healing must have echoed bitterly in his mind. 'A blessing in every household. Are you troubled with bronchitis, asthma, hoarseness…?' Henry Holloway, too, had died the previous year, of bronchitis. The brothers' relationship had never fully healed. Then followed sister Emma, the youngest of the Holloway siblings, at the age of fifty-nine.

Thomas married Jane for love. Her death plunged him into an uncharacteristically demonstrative period of deep mourning, for her and for his lost siblings. He did not leave Tittenhurst for three weeks, partaking of no work, and accepting no visitors but immediate family. A year later, Thomas recorded in his diary, 'This is the 37th anniversary of my marriage with poor dear Jane … I kissed her marble bust today in memory of her.'

It was a harsh loss, all the more so because the college was not yet completed. When Thomas returned to work, he rounded on Crossland for slacking, no doubt anguished by the knowledge that

Jane would never see his greatest triumph completed. Plus, Crossland was carrying on his affair with Eliza Ruth Hatt as openly as he dared. For a man like Thomas, who judged a man's character by how he treated his wife, the architect's behaviour rubbed salt in the wound of his grief. Thomas made it his business to turn up at the college every day, overseeing every aspect of its construction. He must have made a sombre figure, treading the construction site in his mourning garb.

Codes of mourning governed dress and behaviour throughout the nineteenth century. Visual cues such as black-trimmed letter paper helped others to know how to behave towards the bereaved, and formal mores gave those in mourning a sense of order to adhere to in their time of emotional turmoil. For women, there were fine details of clothing to be considered: black lightening to greys and lavenders for those about to re-enter living society. The time they spent in these clothes depended on which family member they mourned. For a middle or upper-class woman, the loss of a husband would trigger a two-year period of mourning in full black weeds, followed by a swift new marriage if she was young and in need of financial support. A youthful, pretty widow was considered a fine bride, whereas older widows were implicitly sexless and untouchable. When Queen Victoria lost her Prince Albert, her extravagant mourning never ended, and was considered an embarrassing overindulgence in sentiment. Mourning garb existed to shelter the widow, not to show off.

For men, the codes were more Spartan. As a widower, Thomas was expected to eschew social events and wear morning clothes for a year – a black suit, black gloves and a black neck-tie, not too strikingly different to his usual daywear. Public shows of emotion were not to be encouraged; as the head of the family, the mourning husband had to steer his dependants by example. Sober forbearance, at least publically, was the order of the day, though there are accounts of grieving men falling apart unexpectedly around friends, especially women, who were expected to offer motherly care despite this breach of etiquette. Loneliness was not considered a healthy state for any Victorian man, and those who had lost their wives were strongly encouraged to get back to work, the sooner the better, for him and his family. But Thomas Holloway had no children. His in-laws, the Drivers and the Martins, took care of business in America and beyond, knowing how hard it was for Thomas to take any time off. The remaining Holloways kept their distance, possibly at his request. Had he been a younger man, he would have been encouraged to find a new wife, in accordance with the assumed need for men to be reassured and supported. Jane's sister, Mary Ann 'Polly' Driver, would have been a suitable candidate; Thomas was fond of her. It wasn't uncommon for dying wives to give permission for their husbands to remarry – even to marry close in-laws – out of a sense of duty to be the caregiver, even in death. But Jane had expired suddenly, and Thomas was in his seventies. What was the use of striving to begin life again? All he had was work.

Emotional shutdown may have been the proper mode of mourning for a man of Thomas's class, but as his diary entry about Jane's statue attests, he was privately deeply wounded. The veneration of objects was one aspect of Victorian mourning that allowed men to vent their feelings. Photographs, statuettes and portraits were, in some sense, comforting reminders of the deceased, but as men were encouraged not to dwell on memories – even pleasant ones – they also served the purpose of opening the gates for grieving in a very private sense. Case studies of Victorian widowers provide a window on a private world of emotion considered incompatible with a man's role in society. One such widower – a doctor, Seth Thompson – found public solace in his religion when his wife passed away after a short illness. However, a deathbed portrait was his lasting talisman: 'Without this drawing I should be infinitely more wretched than I am now for it brings her back to me with such reality that a short time spent in looking at it and praying by it has always a wholesome effect upon my mind.' Thompson intended to have a special locked frame built for the portrait, reinforcing its status as an object for his eyes only – almost a holy thing.

Art held up a mirror to grief, and provided an outlet. The death of 22-year-old poet Arthur Hallam produced one of the nineteenth century's most well-known mourning poems, Alfred Lord Tennyson's 1849 *In Memoriam*. Dark, ornate and enormous, like a piece of Victorian furniture, the poem made a stir for its treatment of the male experience of bereavement, showing a man travelling through the stages of grief for a dear friend in the most personal, most intimate terms:

> *Let Love clasp Grief lest both be drown'd,*
> *Let darkness keep her raven gloss:*
> *Ah, sweeter to be drunk with loss,*
> *To dance with death, to beat the ground,*
>
> *Than that the victor Hours should scorn*
> *The long result of love, and boast,*
> *'Behold the man that loved and lost,*
> *But all he was is overworn.'*

For many, the poem was all too sentimental, agonising over every pang and unanswered question. It was unseemly for a man to revel in melancholy. Even women were cautioned against excessive wallowing, which didn't stop Tennyson himself from being accused of effeminacy. But the poem addressed important questions. Why was there such a disconnect between elaborate Victorian funerary rituals and the personal experience of grief? Was the act of making public the true intensity of one's feelings a kind of betrayal? These questions struck a chord with men, especially. Despite a blossoming industry in sympathy cards festooned with weeping cherubs and syrupy verse, it was when widowers took to spending inordinate time beside their wives' graves that relatives became concerned. Occasionally in such cases, doctors were summoned to assess physical and mental health. For men, healing was not considered as important as the speed of the return to an appearance of normalcy. Therefore, consumption of art was an indirect – and acceptable – tool for men in mourning.

In the widower Alfred Lyttelton's words: 'As you get a little bit away ... one can find in beautiful poetry above all, deeper and more hidden beauties, which no one can quite appreciate without experience of their truth.'

Thomas Holloway's faith, unorthodox as it was, may have offered a little comfort in his time of loss. But to Crossland, Holloway was 'a man who always worked with his head, not his heart'. Action was needed. After three weeks of pained solitude at Tittenhurst, Thomas threw his energy and money into a new project for Crossland to grapple with. The architect, having put up with Thomas's extremely specific demands for so many years, must have been somewhat surprised to be told to stop what he was doing and convert what was originally intended as Holloway College's recreation room into a gallery for pictures. Thomas stipulated the gallery was to be as similar to that of Vassar College as possible. It wasn't ideal. The windows had already been completed, and were awkwardly placed to catch art-viewing light, but Crossland did his best to improvise.

In the early summer of 1881, gossip spread. Someone had spent a veritable fortune on Landseer's ghastly polar bears. *The Times* – which Thomas preferred not to read, having ended up in Whitecross Prison partly because of his debts to them – tattled excitedly:

> The greatest curiosity prevailed and many questions were asked about this new purchaser in the field, and whether the name were not simply a *nom de guerre*. That this was so became the general conclusion, and it was understood that, whatever the real name of the present owner of these fine works, it is to be kept a secret for the present.

It was the largest sum ever spent on a Landseer painting at auction – £6,615, followed by another £12,232 on other paintings on that day alone. The other bidders were blown clean out of the water by this anonymous bidder, represented by Thomas's least recognisable brother-in-law, Henry Driver. 'Splendid extravagance', *The Times* called the purchase. There were more to come. Over the following three years, Christie's was to enjoy the patronage of an anonymous and passionate art collector. Some accused this mysterious individual of inflating prices, but the artists who were still living weren't about to complain; never before had they dreamt of their work fetching such sums.

Why did Thomas want to keep his name out of the press? It wasn't as though he was averse to self-publicity. Other men were happy to announce their new acquisitions, inviting parties of friends to private viewings. Thomas, in his own words, hated to 'beat the big drum' when it came to his personal life, but this reticence, I feel, indicates these paintings were not investments only. Along with *Man Proposes*, Thomas purchased an impressive collection of contemporary works, most of which were decidedly melancholy, if not downright sentimental. There were two Millais paintings – *Princes in The Tower* and *Princess Elizabeth, Daughter of Charles I, In Prison At St James* – both depicting fearful black-clad children who died before adulthood. *Tomb in the Water* is a sombre landscape by William James Muller, who died at just thirty-three. Anthony Vandyke Copley Fielding's *Travellers in A Storm, Approach to Winchester* shows a weary band of pilgrims trudging into a tempest, represented as a black abyss in the centre of the canvass. The collection was expanded over the following years to include examples of social realism with a heavy sentimental gloss: Frank Holl's *Newgate: Committed For Trial*, and Luke Fildes' *Applicants for Admission to a Casual Ward*. These scenes of poverty chime with the Victorian dichotomy of the deserving and undeserving poor; familiar city scenes of rogues and drunkards who have orchestrated their own social downfalls, alongside the innocents brought down with them. Madonna-like wives clutch bundles of wan, hungry children, while jailers do their duty with helpless regret. Such tear-jerkers acted as a moral warning as well as a call to charity.

It was easy to slip through the cracks of Victorian society, just as it was easy to be overcome by the elements of the Arctic. So many of the paintings Thomas collected in the 1880s confirmed what he already knew: human life was a fragile thing.

It is worth noting that, at first, many of the paintings did not hang in the college gallery, but privately in Tittenhurst. Were these grim, sentimental scenes useful to him in his years of widowhood? Did he see something of his own ambition in Franklin's tragic example?

By 1881, Thomas Beecham was a household name as familiar as Holloway. For some time, Holloway's adverts had been clumsily emulating the Beecham slogan – 'Worth a guinea a box!' – with the rather more leaden 'of equal value of the coin of the realm'. The unimaginable was happening: for the first time, Holloway's Pills and Ointment were losing their share of the home market. Marketing outlays were consuming more and more of the years' profits. Beecham, on the other hand, was going from strength to strength. The company Holloway had devoted his life to – and that his dearly missed Jane had devoted hers to in turn – was showing signs of decline. Beecham still had plenty of life in him, and a parade of adult children who would carry his name and business into the twentieth century. It is easy to imagine Thomas sitting alone at home, contemplating Landseer's strangest work of art, amid the melancholy of all things done.

It has been suggested that Thomas purchased art purely as an investment, to increase the college's standing and leave one last gift to the nation by collecting whatever was popular at the time. Indeed, he acquired Frith's hugely admired *The Railway Station*, which he had noticed decades earlier. A steal at the bargain price of £2,000, considering it had originally gone for over £4,000. But the collection, even taken as a purely amateur selection to decorate the college, contained some surprisingly radical messages.

The Banker's Private Room: Negotiating a Loan by John Callcott Horsley depicts a drab banker and a young woman discussing terms across a table. What makes the painting remarkable is how the girl dominates this male space. In her fur-trimmed red garments, she leans across the table, maintaining eye contact with the banker as a man might, yet retaining a mask of feminine coquettishness. In the background, a clerk peeks in at the scene, shocked. An old woman smiles to herself. The dog at the girl's feet is perfectly docile, suggesting the banker, too, will soon do as she commands. Criticised for invading the masculine realm of higher education, the students of Holloway College may well have enjoyed the implications.

Another interesting choice, sharing first place with *Man Proposes, God Disposes* as the most expensive work in the collection, is *The Babylonian Marriage Market* by Edwin Longsden Long. Sold to Thomas for a record-breaking fee in 1882, the painting sits uncomfortably in a Victorian women's college. It depicts a Middle Eastern auction block where young girls wait in order of attractiveness to be allotted a husband. Those considered the prettiest (not coincidentally the most Caucasian) are passive, confident of fetching a high price. On the plain end of the queue, the girls talk and gesticulate, showing their characters, though the plainest hides her face in shame. These girls were to offer dowries to reluctant potential husbands, to make up for their looks. In the painting's centre is the girl considered neither beautiful nor ugly. Her fate was to be given away for free. She stares out at the viewer, calmly confrontational. In nineteenth-century Orientalist fantasies such as this, the female subject's beauty was there to be appraised, and the model was rarely allowed to make eye contact with the viewer – such a thing would unsettle the evaluating male gaze. Without that central figure, *The Babylonian Marriage Market* would be a most peculiar choice for a women's college where the students had cast off traditional gender constraints. As it is, when seen through female eyes, that lone figure, with her back turned to the men, could well be interpreted as a sly riposte to the abuse 'bluestockings' were accustomed to. The students had, for now at least, wisely rejected the marriage market, taking their destinies into their own hands. The presence of the painting in the college was an interesting vote of confidence – these weren't delicate young girls who needed sheltering from racy pictures. They were capable of critical thinking.

Man Proposes, God Disposes did not ultimately reside in the picture gallery. Curiously – or perhaps as someone's idea of a joke – it was hung in the exam hall, quickly gaining a reputation as an omen of bad luck. Students dreaded being sat next to the grim scene for fear of flunking, and eventually talk of 'the curse' led to the tradition of draping the bears in the Union Jack at exam time. By strange coincidence, one of the archaeologists who discovered the sunken wreck of one of Franklin's lost ships in 2014 took her exams beside the veiled painting.

Whatever their purpose or meaning, the paintings were a great gift. Modern art for a modern college. Vassar, Holloway's American mirror image, had purchased his pictures for his own college for $20,000. True to his word, Thomas 'beat Vassar into fits', spending a total of about £100,000 on art as a gift to the nation. To put this into perspective, his total profits for 1880 were just over £20,000. No other college in Britain boasted such a fine collection of modern art. When Thomas dropped the *nom du guerre,* the *Art Journal* eulogised him as a surprise latecomer to the world of art, but nevertheless an incredibly impressive collector. What a collection he could have amassed had he thrown his hat into the ring earlier! Queen Victoria herself wrote in her diary of the 'fine specimens' on show. She even liked Long's *Marriage Market.* The picture gallery was the crowning glory of the lavish labour of love that was Holloway College. Further funds were ploughed into scholarships, and it was estimated that the college alone represented £600,000 of personal investment. For John Betjeman, the two Holloway buildings were the most amazing in the land: 'Once seen they haunt the mind like a recurring and exciting dream.'

The college was to be Jane's memorial. It was she who had urged him to do something for women, and like Thomas's mother before her, Jane's steadfast support had been a great comfort to her husband. For forty years they had stayed true to each other, and as a final act of dedication, Thomas had a statue of Jane made for the college, sitting by his side as she did in life. It's a touching composition, with Jane sitting like a patient monarch while Thomas sweeps his arm to show her what he has built for her. There is a great deal of affection present. Neither subject is especially idealised; Jane is slightly dumpy in her neat dress, and Thomas starting to go bald. The statue puts Jane – and by extension, the whole female sex – literally at the centre of the college. Thomas's gesture was an invitation to the future. For a young student eager to improve herself and put her brain to use, being welcomed by such a sight must have been exciting. Perhaps the grand surroundings soothed a little of the frustration at not being welcome in Oxbridge. For Thomas, the completed college momentarily eased his grief. In an uncharacteristically unguarded moment, he is said to have looked around him at the Gothic splendour, patted Crossland on the back, and said, 'Well done, Mister Crossland. I am more than pleased.'

Thomas did not live to see the grand opening of the college or the sanatorium. The morbid fixations of his twilight years seem to have anticipated his absence at what should have been his moment of triumph. Thomas died on 26 December 1883, at his home, of a similar bronchial infection as his dear Jane. When he was still strong enough to write, he noted down this similarity with a touch of his old arch humour. He refused the help of doctors – sceptical of them to the last – and most definitely did not resort to his own remedies. He was buried alongside Jane, with the epitaph: 'He being dead yet speaketh.'

Sheltering from the sun under her mourning parasol, Queen Victoria officially opened Holloway College on 30 June 1886. It was an occasion of great celebration, attended by hundreds of journalists and hopeful young women watching the future roll out in front of their eyes. Jane would surely have been beaming.

Chapter 13

Picking the Bones

How to eulogise a quack who transformed himself into one of the nation's greatest benefactors? On news of his death, *The Illustrated London News* printed Thomas's portrait, looking stern as an elder statesman. As a popular weekly paper that happily advertised patent medicines, the editors were content to embrace the duality of Thomas's life without much critical commentary:

> Mr Thomas Holloway, the well-known manufacturer of patent medicines, died of bronchitis at his residence, Tittenhurst, near Sunningdale, Berks, on Wednesday week, at the advanced age of eighty-four. His name will long be remembered for the munificence which he showed in the closing years of his life.

But this was not a man universally loved. In 1877, *The Standard* in Winnipeg received an advertising leaflet from Holloway, and responded publically:

> Everywhere mankind swallows this medicated poison ... Having been splendidly remunerated for circulating these drug-poisons, Mr Holloway is going to 'compound for sins he has a mind-to' by erecting a college for women ... If his performances equal his promises, Mr Holloway will certainly do more good in spending his money than he did in making it.

But he had. And on his death, the press couldn't help but show admiration. *The Times* said:

The last few days of December have brought a noteworthy addition to the obituary list of the year. The London Stock Exchange is already in a flutter at the news. Mr Holloway's fortune has been the accumulation of a long lifetime. He has grown rich by his own exertion, and in a certain sense in spite of himself, for very few men have made a more gracious and free handed use of their money as he has.

It was the princely gift of the college and sanatorium for which he would be remembered, but his legacy was inescapably entangled with the regrettable business of patent medicine. In Holloway's case, *The Times* were careful to say, no one had been known to die as a result of taking the pills or applying the ointment. Such were the standards. It would have been all too much fun for the press had Holloway been a lover of the high life, throwing his fortune away on gambling and extravagant clothes, like Baron Spolasco and his nefarious ilk. But Holloway's decision to dedicate himself to philanthropy, while not a complete change of heart, did deny the press a solid soapbox for protesting the patent medicine trade on the event of his death. *Punch* and Thackeray, of course, would be dissenting voices for years to come, but what made Holloway fascinating to his contemporaries was that he had interrupted the narrative of the wicked, wealthy quack. *The Times* obituary reads rather feebly, almost brushing off the pills as a means to a greater end:

On the intrinsic merits of these much vaunted drugs we cannot pretend to be informed. If they possessed one tenth part of the wonderful virtues which have been assigned to them, their discovery may safely be set down as marking an era of no small importance in the curative art ... The praises of his medicines have been sounded in all lands and in all known languages. Every available place, from London boarding house to the great Pyramid has been pressed into the service, and been forced to bear testimonial to their merits.

> [Holloway was] one of that remarkable class which seemed destined to become rich, who roll wealth together in a way which ordinary men fail either to follow or to understand ... To these men money comes like the good gifts of fairies in our childhood tales.

Like a conjurer, Thomas had turned kitchen oil into gold. But now the conjurer was dead, and like the gossips at Scrooge's funeral, all the public cared about was where his remaining fortune was going.

Thomas had been well aware of the ugly scramble for money his death would inevitably trigger. Before he died, he had the unenviable task of dividing his fortune amongst his relatives, and had initially left modestly large gifts to his surviving siblings, along with control of the business to his solicitor. In the wake of Jane's death, Thomas had to completely rethink his legacy. Of Thomas's blood relations, few still lived, and those who did were kept at arm's length. Brother Henry had died the previous decade, and sister Mary Jane was working for Thomas with her husband in America. Caroline, widowed at fifty, had already enjoyed financial support from Thomas and was angling for more on his death. Where once he had hoped to give Jane as much comfort and security as she could ever need, the thought of posthumously funding Cousin Willie's theatrical ambitions was unappealing. In total, Thomas redrafted his will three times amid the pressure of speculation – what lucky individual would inherit the Holloway riches? In total, it came to almost £600,000. A king's ransom.

First, he made provision for his staff. To his late wife's servants, he had already left a lump sum of £300 on top of an annual annuity of £30 each, signing off with the wish they would both live long and happy lives. 'What a good and kind friend you have been to us,' the girls responded.

As for his own employees, in 1877, he handed out generous bonuses for all, and raises for some. It isn't known if Mister Rough was still around to take his share, but a surviving letter shows the affection of the Holloway staff for their employer:

We, the Clerks of your establishment, beg more heartily to thank
you for the present so kindly made us in commemoration of this,
the fortieth anniversary of the commencement of your business;
which permits us to hope may long continue to flourish and be
guided by that hand which has hitherto controlled it with such
marvellous success.

In tendering you our sincere thanks and congratulations, we wish
you health and happiness.

Twenty-two signatures followed. Most of these came from employees
of many years' standing, even decades. Thomas had seen them
flourish, marry, and start families, and had always taken a genuine
interest in their welfare. Thomas was a good man to work for, even
if the product was ethically questionable.

The business seemed to matter more to George Martin and
Henry Driver than to Thomas at the time of his third and final
will. Previously, his executors had been instructed to continue
the business for another ten years to avoid dropping the staff
into sudden unemployment. Both Martin and Driver had since
adopted the Holloway surname; a touching gesture, and proof of
their commitment to the firm. They had, after all, been practically
running the company for a decade or so while Thomas had ploughed
his energy into the college and sanatorium. Thomas had stipulated
that neither institution was to bring in profit. The business, the
shares and the investments were what everyone had their eye on.

To Caroline's horror, the fortune she and her son had spent years
setting their hopes on slipped through her fingers. Thomas's late
wife's sister, Mary Ann Driver, inherited practically everything: the
money, the estate, and even the business. An additional £50,000
was left to his and Jane's adopted daughter, Celia. She was set for
life. Mary Ann, being unmarried, would enjoy total security, and a
say in the direction of the business, which was tacitly intended to
be divided between George Martin and Henry Driver. It seemed
Thomas truly did prefer the Drivers and the Martins to his own

kin. The Holloways were sure there was some mistake. A court date loomed for the spring.

Caroline, incensed that she and Willie were cut off, claimed she had been exiled from Tittenhurst since 1881, and that Thomas had been completely in the hands of the Driver family. His habits over the past fifteen years, she said, had become peculiar. Perhaps the will was not written in sound mind.

Those who knew Thomas found it hard to believe he had ever submitted to the control of anyone, let alone lose his wits. This was the man who had a lifelong habit of noting down how many of his pennies were spent on candles. He worked at a pace that would have licked a man half his age hollow. A surgeon came forward to attest that when Thomas had been diagnosed with heart failure and chronic congestion of the lungs, he had been completely lucid. The presence of a physician made the defending solicitor laugh – Professor Holloway evidently had little faith in his own healing genius.

It was unlikely that the Drivers had held Thomas hostage all these years. But Thomas's decision to hand over practically everything to his sister-in-law was a puzzling one. Faced with the indignant figure of Caroline Young, elderly, well dressed and concerned for her late brother's welfare, the court was surprised to learn that Thomas had been sending both Caroline and his other surviving sister, Mary Jane, an annual allowance of £150. Caroline tried to argue that because Mary Ann now had control of these funds, she and her fatherless son were left in a precarious position. Indeed, leaving such a gargantuan sum to a single sister-in-law was a rather unorthodox move when Thomas's own sisters were waiting in the wings. What brother in his right mind would have made this decision?

It turned out that not only was Mary Ann Driver willingly still sending these yearly sums to both women, she had also already sent a lump sum of £5,000 to the widowed Caroline. Extremely generous of her, considering the two women barely knew one another.

But Caroline argued she needed more. To her dismay, it was then that Willie's wayward behaviour came to light. In his own words, Thomas had been forced to pay a doctor to 'manufacture' sick notes to excuse Willie's absences at the bank. Cutting Willie's allowance when he abandoned his wife and children to try his luck on the London stage was the only decent and sensible course of action, and although the harsh tactic had worked and the family now had a butcher shop of their own, Willie was once again scuttling away to the theatres with his daughter Georgiana. Bachelor behaviour in a married man was frowned upon, particularly when it came about as a result of feelings of entitlement. True to the Victorian melodrama narrative, the blame would lay at the feet of the mother, who, rather than using her own inheritance to keep her son on the straight and narrow, was playing the victim out of greed.

Caroline claimed she was in possession of two letters that would prove her deservingness, but the more she protested, the feebler her arguments sounded. Where were these letters? She was reluctant to produce them. When more of Willie's past in the legal profession was revealed, as well as his not-so-legal pastime of exploiting loopholes, Caroline grew less coherent. It became increasingly obvious that Willie had fabricated the letters, and had most likely pressured his elderly mother into going to court in the first place. The penalties for perjury were steep, and Caroline sensibly shut up.

The court found in favour of the defendants. If Thomas Holloway could be held up as an example of a man grown prosperous through his own brainpower and determination, Cousin Willie was his total antithesis, and his self-entitled attitude would not be tolerated. Mary Ann Driver stated she intended to keep up the annual payments of £150 to both Caroline and Mary Jane Holloway. Caroline, at least, took the moral judgement seriously, and put her portion of the money into a trust fund for Willie's children, bypassing him completely.

Though Thomas never lived to see his two mighty gifts to the nation officially opened, he died gratified by the knowledge of what lay ahead. The sanatorium was practically finished in 1878 but not open to patients for another seven years, owing to the college taking precedent, plus Jane's death and Thomas's decline. By the time it did open, the sanatorium was vastly over the original budget: five times per patient what a public asylum built to the Commissioners in Lunacy's standards would cost. It raised the bar for British mental healthcare. Thomas's decision that no self-referred individual could stay more than twelve months was a wise one – the place was so pleasant, some of the patients treated the sanatorium like a holiday home.

Henry Driver-Holloway and George Martin-Holloway took on administration duties, delegating management of the staff to medical superintendent Dr Rees Phillips. Rees Phillips thought highly of his female staff in particular, praising their tact, kindliness, and capacity for the hard and emotionally draining work of overseeing an asylum. Robust physical health was something he valued in employees, just as much as a good education, and so the female staff members were held to a much more modern standard of conduct and ability. Rees Phillips knew there were some asylum tasks male attendants could not – or would not – go near. In the book of case notes, these wormen can be glimpsed in photographs holding rowdy lady patients still, such as Miss Constance Beatrice Coddington, who refused to stop jumping and singing incoherent songs. Propriety meant that men were only ever used to restrain women in extreme cases. The fashionable Victorian ideal of delicacy and deference was no more tolerated at Holloway Sanatorium than at Holloway College. A stout heart was required, and the female attendants of Holloway almost always delivered.

George Martin-Holloway was knighted in 1887 for his work at the sanatorium, an accolade perhaps Thomas himself could have enjoyed, had he lived a little longer. Lord Shaftesbury, whose knowledge and contacts had been instrumental to Thomas's vision, only outlived him by two years. Deaf and riddled with gout, he, too, died of congestion of the lungs. The poor and disadvantaged people he spent his life championing flocked to watch his coffin on its way to Westminster Abbey. Before his death, Shaftesbury remarked that the new, modernised treatment of the mentally ill, such as a patient could receive at Holloway Sanatorium, was 'without any exception the greatest triumph of skill and humanity that the world ever saw.'

As for the college, it was a new dawn for young women. Twenty-three-year-old Constance Maynard had a strictly Evangelical upbringing, free from the wickedness of novels and parties. On her first lone train journey, a fellow traveller opened her eyes to the possibility of an education all of her own:

> It was a new world to me. I asked what 'Tripos' meant and how the students lived and a few other questions; and as we talked, a quiet suggestion arose in my heart as clear as a whisper from without. 'There, that is what you have been waiting for.' Aloud I said 'How interesting! How I would like to go!' – adding mentally in response to the voice, 'Yes, yes, I won't disobey my parents in the least thing, but oh I'll move heaven and earth to get there.'

There was still a terribly long way to go. Most of the women enrolled in the early years of Holloway College were not especially political or radical in their outlook, by their own admission. But what they lacked in direction, they made up for in enthusiasm, and they would need that enthusiasm for drowning out their critics.

> *There is a New Woman, and what do you think?*
> *She lives upon nothing but Foolscap and Ink!*
> *But, though Foolscap and Ink form the whole of her diet,*
> *This nagging New Woman can never be quiet.*
> *Punch,* 1894

For Constance Maynard and her fellow students, foolscap and ink were a diet they were thankful for every day. In 1891, the writer Walter Shaw-Sparrow recalled the simplicity of his grandmother's generation, expected to do little more than mend socks and perhaps write pretty words of little substance. Rudimentary rote knowledge had always been the zenith of academic achievement for women, he noted, but no more. Unlike the men at *Punch*, Shaw-Sparrow was pleased, both for The New Woman and the men who had hitherto seen their education as a birthright of their sex, and would now have to pull their socks up:

> The most important revolution which has taken place during this last half-century in the social life of England is surely that intellectual revolution which women have worked for themselves, and which has done much to unsettle the long-standing belief about the inferiority of the feminine intellect when compared with that of man. The late successes of lady students in competitive examinations, indeed, very convincingly prove that there is no study too difficult for our sisters to follow, not only with advantage to themselves, but, in many cases, with humiliation to us.

The world was changing, thankful in some small part to Thomas Holloway. Queen Victoria authorised the new name, Royal Holloway College, and in 1900 it merged with the University London. Today, the college remains a working university, practically unchanged since its creation, though it now admits male students. The twentieth-century art and architecture critic Sir Nikolaus Pevsner wrote that for all its unfashionable Gothic verve, the building possesses a justified self-confidence, and that Crossland's execution of the Holloway vision there and at the sanatorium represent 'the summit of High Victorian design'.

But what of the pills and ointment, and the dear old firm? The popular rumour was that Thomas's family had squabbled so lengthily over money, there was none left for advertising. This wasn't true, but without the Professor's single-minded shrewdness to guide them, Henry Driver-Holloway and George Martin-Holloway found themselves overwhelmed. For many years, Thomas had been making most of his money through investments and stocks

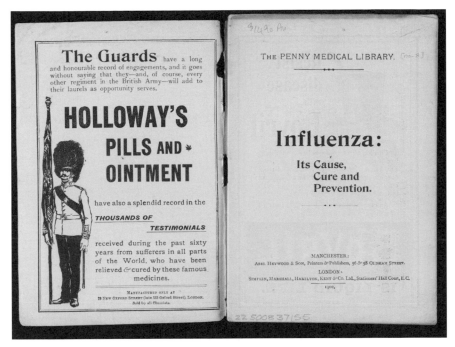

37. A Holloway's ad from 1909. In the wake of Thomas's death, his brothers-in-law tried
to keep up with advertising trends.
(Wellcome Library, London)

rather than patent medicine, and he had duly left these stocks to
both brothers-in-law in the hope they would use them wisely. But
the company had Thomas's name on it. It bore his face. It was
a matter of family pride to keep it afloat, not to mention all the
loyal members of staff who had grown comfortable with Thomas's
firm but fair style of leadership – they had families, after all, and
Thomas had known most of them by name.

Other firms weren't half as good to work for, though they did
provide inspiration in other respects. For twenty years following
the Professor's demise, Henry Driver-Holloway worked hard to
ensure the Holloway packaging and advertising mimicked the more
modern style of Beecham's pills. Collectable Holloway ephemera
was produced bearing the Queen's dour face, possibly in the hope

of hinting at non-existent royal endorsement. The lists of deadly ailments were toned down, replaced by a more optimistic message of 'health assurance' – prophylactics for the modern man and woman. For Beecham's in particular, the image of outdoorsy vigour was selling better than the old Victorian whiff of the sickroom and the morgue. Henry emulated this as best he could, though he couldn't help but add, 'These famous remedies have been in constant use for nearly THREE QUARTERS OF A CENTURY, and are priceless in every emergency of sudden sickness or accident.' The older generations might still respond to a touch of old-fashioned terror.

Thomas Holloway had once hoped the college and sanatorium would act as giant billboards for his wares, but in reality the opposite was happening. In the wake of Thomas's death, other patent medicines were creeping onto his patch: Bile Beans, Dr Williams' Pink Pills, and even Barrett's Mandrake Embrocation with its bottle depicting a duck with a gentleman's head. Barrett's remedy promised to cure 'instantly' the Russian influenza epidemic of 1889, despite being originally touted as relief for bruises. Even The Poor Man's Friend was doing far from poorly – James Beach, who took over the business in the 1880s, became the Mayor of Bridport. Patent medicine on the whole continued to be little more than fat and sugar with powdered flavouring thrown in for good luck, but as George and Henry were coming to discover, the mark of a successful quack was tenacity. With the college and the sanatorium to take care of, and lacking Thomas Holloway's almost supernatural energy, all those pills were a burden they struggled to bear.

Though it's undeniable that the quack medicine trade was – and continues to be – a deplorable exploitation of the vulnerable and desperate, there's a certain sad inevitability to the decline of the Holloway company. Letters from the final members of staff read almost tragically. Those old timers who knew Thomas were genuinely heartsick that their benevolent employer's life's work was coming to an end. The 1880s saw profits dwindle to a third, despite Henry's efforts to modernise the brand. The opulent Oxford Street premises were becoming surplus to requirements. In 1909, when the lease ran out, Henry wrote to Thomas Beecham's son Joseph, unsubtly begging him to purchase the business. Beecham turned him down, and the Holloway staff moved to smaller premises among the industrial chimneys of the far less salubrious Southwark.

The Beecham family had in fact been imitating a few Holloway tactics, particularly the music sheets Thomas once handed out for performance in low theatres and pubs. Beecham, naturally, did it with a wink, attempting a parody of Gilbert and Sullivan's *The Flowers That Bloom in the Spring*: 'The pimples that bloom in the spring, tra la, make such a mess of your face.' But where Holloway had failed to engage Charles Dickens for a little harmless product placement, Beecham's wildly successful fiction omnibuses featured new stories by the giant of literature, as well as by Washington Irving. Beecham's liked to pretend they never paid for testimonials, but when a poor ship's carpenter returned alive from an 1896 expedition to the North Pole, Beecham's were glad to widely distribute his claim that he never had a moment of illness in the Arctic, all thanks to Beecham's pills. Helpfully for Beecham's, that expedition was not a repetition of the Franklin debacle.

For Henry Driver-Holloway and George Martin-Holloway, all these parallels with their late brother-in-law only served to highlight the Holloway company's slow death. And slow it was. Beecham's finally took it over in 1930, twenty-one years after Henry made his humiliating plea. Shortly after writing that letter, Henry had died aged seventy-nine, having been ill and in pain for some time. He had done his best, keeping the company alive for more than double the years Thomas wished. The descendants of Holloway's more modern rival were taking their own company into an area Thomas himself had never displayed much interest in: genuine pharmaceuticals. By that time, Beecham's was one of the market leaders, and the company remains successful today for its cold remedies, despite their fears the

NHS would wipe them out. Holloway's was taken over in 1931, and the pills and ointment continued to be manufactured for a spell at the old London factory under the Veno Drug Company. Veno was another recently acquired concern of Beecham's, run by William Reynard Varney, a cabin boy turned quack. Under Beecham's, the Veno Company churned out various patent medicines bought up by the larger company. Varney later attempted to leave the patent medicine business, but shot himself during financial troubles. Holloway's Pills and Ointment officially ceased to be in 1951, just over a hundred years after Thomas Holloway's first opened for business on the Strand.

It was a slow, dwindling death, painful to those who had seen the Professor's rise to riches. A letter written in 1932 by Henry Driver-Holloway's son of the same name possibly says more about Thomas Holloway's enduring image and personality than any other document:

> I am writing this alone after the turmoil of the last month or so has passed and it is the last day of '113' under the rule of 'Thomas Holloway'. The old servants, many of them over thirty years' service (one was sixty-seven years with us) have had to pay the penalty of my ill-success and have been discharged, for Modern Business knows little of the tender emotions which swayed Mr Holloway at all times to take the liveliest interest in his dependants, keen, hard 'business' man though he was.

Henry and his family were desperate for money. Against all his remaining personal pride, he hoped the sanatorium would grant him a small loan to live on.

> When a man gets really down, somehow or other, friends seem to lose interest … I have not been very wise, I have been dogged by quite a bit of misfortune, but in the business world my brother and I have through many a bad trying time kept the name of 'Thomas Holloway' clean and of good repute.

Henry was 'hurt and distressed beyond measure' that the company would wither under his command. He hoped to support the remaining servants and one impoverished Holloway nephew as a final tribute to the old, personal way of doing business, when a job was for life. But by the end of April 1932, some of the remaining staff, ageing and ailing, were forced to fall on parish relief. The final throes of the firm can't help but resemble Landseer's polar bears tearing apart Franklin's ambitions.

A final shaky statement in the letter book reads, '6 years' service and no one seems to care.'

Chapter 14

He Being Dead Yet Speaketh

Thomas Holloway was my first cousin, five times removed. My great-great-great-great grandfather, William Holloway, was Thomas Holloway senior's brother, born in 1781. My cousin had little to no knowledge of his own lineage. In the 1940s, when college staff looked into the origins of the Holloway coat of arms stamped variously about the campus, it was discovered that the Holloways were 'of lowly descent, barely yeoman class' and Thomas himself didn't know the Christian name of his own grandfather. The coat of arms was a fabrication, as was the family motto, *nil desperandum*. But Thomas's wealth, coupled with the expanding class boundaries of the mid-nineteenth century, allowed him to invent his own place in the world; something that had scarcely been possible for his father's generation, let alone his lowly yeoman grandfather.

Pursuing an interest in the Victorians, I was long aware of an eminent 'Uncle Thomas' character, but the link between Holloway College and that nebulous figure never clicked until recently. Uncovering the extent of Thomas's vast wealth was all the more astonishing knowing that my own great-grandparents couldn't afford their own gravestone. Having distanced himself from most of his blood relatives, I wonder if my branch of the Holloways even knew of their successful cousin, let alone hoped for a slice of his riches when he died.

My branch of the Holloways are still seafarers, still an average of 6 feet, with a hint of Thomas's features still discernible in the brow. What I glimpsed of my cousin's private self, I liked, and sometimes recognised, especially his wry sense of humour. One story tells of a business associate commenting over dinner that the wine Thomas served him was so good, he could have happily been paid with it. Thomas chose to take that statement literally, sending him crates of the stuff in lieu of money.

I've tried to present my ancestor without too much modern judgement. Had he left behind more personal papers, or been more sociable, perhaps my task would have been easier, but my own goal was to ascertain why he did what he did, and what he felt about it. Thomas made outrageous claims and an unimaginable amount of money from his pills and ointment, but he never mocked the people who bought them. He believed in the placebo effect and always maintained the testimonials he received from grateful customers were genuine. Perhaps that was the placebo effect working in reverse.

Thomas's actions show him as a man of contradictions. Despite spending decades as Professor Holloway, the healing genius, it was rumoured he declined a baronetcy from the Queen. 'Beating the big drum,' as he put it, was faintly uncomfortable when not wearing the hat of the Professor. Despite his immense wealth, he lived a quiet life. Most surprising were Thomas's radical leanings. Where they came from and why, he left few clues. To allow himself to be guided by women activists in planning the college – to the point that it annoyed his male colleagues – gives an interesting insight into his character. Ruthless in business, he nonetheless knew when to step back for the greater good. Still, his attitude towards charity was very typical of his time; dividing people into categories of the deserving and the undeserving poor. While he could be exceedingly generous in gifts and loans to those he was fond of, one step wrong and Thomas would withdraw his support – or threaten to. Quite often, despite himself, his heart was still swayed by a sad story. His own youthful foolishness in feuding with Albinolo could well have been the source of these high standards as well as the sympathy he tried hard to conceal. While other successful quacks lived the high life, Thomas was strangely abstemious, even frugal, suggesting he applied his philosophy of self-control as much to himself as others.

The temptation to paint Thomas as a straightforward swindler simply doesn't fit, though many of his contemporaries tried. However, *Punch's* frustration at the seemingly unstoppable patent medicine trade struck a chord with me. Where there is desperation, there will be those willing to exploit it for profit. Many times in researching this book, I stumbled upon modern quacks promising to reverse blindness with a herb, or cure tinnitus with drops taken on the tongue. Victorians are sometimes portrayed as naïve, led into danger by the razzmatazz of showmanship over science. But questionable health fads and misinformation prevail today, even with mass communication. For an ordinary working person in the nineteenth century, with no safety net of social security and no funds for a qualified physician, it's little wonder patent medicine was one of the first ports of call in times of sickness. From a cold business point of view, the industry was a goldmine. Though I never felt Thomas Holloway was in the same league as reckless killers like Baron Spolasco, it is nonetheless sobering to see quacks continue to scratch out an existence on the backs of the sick.

Thomas came into business at precisely the right time. After his death, into the dawn of the twentieth century, patent medicine companies began to feel the encroaching presence of the law. In 1919, the British Government set up the Department of Health and set about the difficult task of regulating patent medicines. A Select Committee was set up, and it was agreed that those wishing to sell proprietary medicines should submit ingredients, packaging and proven effects for scrutiny, after which they would be granted membership to the Association of Manufacturers of British Proprietaries. Anyone claiming cures for incurable diseases would be barred from membership. The word 'cure' was still permitted in advertising, however, providing it did not imply magical success as so many Victorian elixirs did.

This wasn't the death knell, however. The existence of the association did not lead to a Parliamentary Act. These were guidelines to help savvy consumers. Inconsistency in advertising continued, and the *it's worth a try* attitude unfortunately prevailed amongst the ailing public. The Pharmacy and Medicines Act of 1942 brought in controls on advertising of remedies for certain diseases, using the codes set down by the Association of Manufacturers of British Proprietaries as guidelines. Truly, it was the introduction of the National Health Service that did the most damage to the patent medicine trade. Finally, the working classes could receive decent healthcare without risking poverty. Many companies folded after the NHS's inception in 1948, and more followed. Prominent proprietary medicine companies like Beecham's were forced to enter legitimacy to survive, or, like Burgess' Lion Ointment, admit they were for cosmetic use only. Today, Holloway's Ointment would make a perfectly serviceable scented hand cream.

The decline of Holloway's Pills & Ointment after Thomas's death, I believe, would not have troubled him. The college and the sanatorium were the achievements Thomas wished to be remembered for, and at the time of their conception, he already showed signs of losing interest in quackery. He took the jibes of Dickens, Thackeray and *Punch* in his stride, but the turnaround from quack to philanthropist was not a decision he made in order to improve his image. He could have simply bankrolled the college, but I believe that his decision to make time to meet and listen to women like Elizabeth Garrett-Anderson and Maria Grey shows him to be a surprisingly forward-thinking man, and one committed to social change, even if that sentiment did not extend to the patent medicine trade. In the creation of the two institutions, he chose to give beautiful buildings laudable and progressive purposes, rather than settling on impressive facades. In this sense, his philanthropy was quite the opposite of his medicines. It would have satisfied him to know the evidence of his generosity remains long after the pills and puffery have gone.

It has been said that Thomas Holloway exemplified the Victorian hope that tomorrow would be better than today. But that sounds like the Professor talking. In Thomas's own words, he wished to do something for coming generations, in his own little way. I think he would have been more than pleased.

Acknowledgements

Many people have helped and encouraged me during the creation of *The Mighty Healer*.

I first want to thank the Holloways – my dad, Peter and Auntie Pauline – who fostered my interest in history and have always supported me in my endeavours. My partner, Gabriel, has been brilliant throughout this entire process. Thanks go to him for beautifully photographing and editing my collection of artefacts and ephemera. He deserves admiration for putting up with all my horrible dinnertime anecdotes about mercury poisoning.

Special thanks go to Helen, Ignacio, Gerlinde, Madeleine, Joan and Keith, Claire, and Kylie, and many more of my friends for all their generous support and encouragement. The same goes to the online historian community, particularly the many histmed bloggers with all their expertise and enthusiasm.

Last and certainly not least, I must thank the archive staff of Holloway College and the Surrey History Centre who have been so helpful. The Wellcome Trust also has my gratitude for making so much of their archive open to independent scholars.

Bibliography

By no means an exhaustive list, these are some of my most used sources, which may be useful for anyone wishing to further explore the topics discussed in *The Mighty Healer*.

Books and pamphlets

Bingham, Caroline, *The History of Royal Holloway College, 1880–1986*, Constable, London, 1987.

Clarke, Edward, *Sex in Education*, Houghton, Mifflin & Co, Boston, 1873.

Coghln, Francis, *A guide to France, explaining every form and expense from London to Paris*, J. Onwhyn, London, 1830.

Corley, T.A.B., *Beecham's, 1848–2000: from Pills to Pharmaceuticals*, Crucible Books, London, 2011.

Cramp, Arthur J., *Nostrums and Quackery*, Press of American Medical Association, Chicago, 1872.

Doherty, Francis, *A Study in Eighteenth-Century Advertising Methods: The Anodyne Necklace*, Edwin Mellen Press Ltd, London, 1993.

Ellis, Sarah Stickney, *The Daughters of England, their position in society, character and responsibilities*, D. Appleton, New York, 1842.

Flanders, Judith, *The Victorian City: Everyday Life in Dickens' London*, Atlantic Books, London, 2012.

Granville, Joseph Mortimer, *The Care and Cure of the Insane*, Hardwick & Bogue, London, 1877.

Gunn, John C., *Gunn's Domestic Medicine, or Poor Man's Friend*, John M. Gallagher Printer, Ohio, 1835.

Harrison-Barbet, Anthony, *Thomas Holloway: Victorian Philanthropist*, Royal Holloway, University of London, 1994.

Jalland, Pat, *Death in the Victorian Family*, Oxford University Press, 1996.

Maas, Jeremy, *Victorian Taste: Complete Catalogue of Paintings at the Royal Holloway College*, A. Zwemmer Ltd, London, 1982.

Martin, Jane, *Women and the Politics of Schooling in Victorian and Edwardian England*, Leicester University Press, London, 1999.

More Secret Remedies, What They Cost and What They Contain, Press of British Medical Association, London, 1912.

Patrick Elliott, John, *Palaces, Patronage and Pills: Thomas Holloway, His Sanatorium, College and Picture Gallery*, Royal Holloway, University of London, 1996.

Perceval, John, *A Narrative of the Treatment Experienced by a Gentleman, During a State of Mental Derangement*, Effingham Wilson, London, 1840.

Porter, Roy (ed), *The Faber Book of Madness*, Faber, London, 1991.

Porter, Roy, *Quacks: Fakers & Charlatans in English Medicine*, NPI Media Group, London, 2000.

Potter, Nathaniel Potter, *An essay on the medicinal properties and deleterious qualities of arsenic*, William W. Woodward, 1796.

Purvis, June, *A History of Women's Education in England: Women and Political Society in Victorian Britain*, Clarendon Press, Oxford, 1991.

Rance, Caroline, *The Quack Doctor: Historical Remedies for all your Ills*, History Press, Stroud, 2013.

Robinson, Jane, *Bluestockings*, Penguin Viking, London, 2009.

Sanders, Valerie, *Eve's Renegades: Victorian Anti-Feminist Women Novelists*, Macmillan Press, London, 1996.

Secret Remedies, What They Cost and What They Contain, Press of British Medical Association, London, 1909.

Shepherd, Anna, *Institutionalizing the Insane in Nineteenth-Century England*, Routledge, London, 2014.

Thackeray, William Makepeace, *Thackerayana*, Chatto & Windus, Piccadilly, 1875.

Vickery, Margaret Birney, *Buildings for Bluestockings: The Architecture and Social History of Women's Colleges in Late Victorian England*, Associated University Presses, London, 1999.

Young, James Harvey, *The Toadstool Millionaires: A Social History of Patent Medicines in America Before Federal Regulation*, Princeton University Press, 2015.

Wise, Sarah, *Inconvenient People*, Vintage, London, 2012.

Newspapers and periodicals

'A Horrid Blue-Stocking', *Cork Examiner*, 23 December 1857.

'A Very Strange Story', *Glasgow Herald*, 18 June 1872.

Burra Record, 25 November 1881.

'Caution to the Public', *Gloucestershire Chronicle*, 15 September 1838.

Dublin Evening Packet and Correspondent, 14 December 1848.

'Echoes of the Week', *The Illustrated London News*, 5 January 1884.

'English Old Maids', *Dundee Evening Telegraph*, 21 November 1884.

'Famed Throughout the World!' *New Zealander*, 28 October 1848.

'Fine Arts. The Royal Academy', *The Athenaeum*, 7 May 1864.

'Holloway VS Holloway – Injunction', *Lincolnshire Chronicle*, 13 December 1850.

'Holloway's Medicines in America', *The Chemist & Druggist*, 15 December 1881.

'Puff Pantomime', *Punch*, Vol. 10, 1848.

'Rolls Court', *North Wales Chronicle*, 16 November 1850.

'The American's Friend', *New-Orleans Commercial Bulletin*, 28 March 1855.

'The Arctic Expedition', *The Times*, 23 October 1854.

'The Billstickers Exhibition', *Punch*, 9 May 1847.

'The Last of the Quacks', *Cork Examiner*, 5 November 1858.

'The Late Mister T. Holloway', *The Illustrated London News*, 5 January 1884.

'The Panacea Proclaimed!', *Punch*, 10 January 1863.
The Times, 30 May 1881.
'There Are None of Us Safe', *Punch*, July to December, 1848.
'Sir Samuel Baker's Medical Practice', *The Chemist & Druggist*,
    14 December 1867.

Websites

Katz, Leslie, *Dickens and Product Placement: Did He Refuse an
    Offer from 'Professor' Holloway?* 2015, *http://www.ssrn.com/en/*
Reynolds, G.W.M., *Mysteries of London*, http://www.victorianlondon.
    org/mysteries/mysteries-00-introduction.htm

Artifacts

Holloway Sanatorium patient records: Wellcome Collection
Thomas Holloway's miscellaneous letters and diaries: Surrey History
    Centre

Index